*R*osemary Reed Miller in her book, *Threads of Time, The Fabric of History*, pays tribute to American women of color who have supported and sustained themselves and their families through the creative use of their hands and fabric.

The contributions of the work of women such as Elizabeth Keckley during the Lincoln presidency and Anne Lowe in the Kennedy era should be brought to the attention of the public, especially to the young people of today whose parents and ancestors make clothes for them or sew for a living.

As a daughter and grand-daughter of three such talented women (mother sewed for each of her seven daughters and our grandmothers taught sewing and sewed for others), I applaud Reed Miller for honoring some of the seamstresses whose expertise with "needle and thread" has clothed many and influenced fashion for centuries.

I enjoyed reading *Threads of Time* because five generations of my family have lived and labored in the nation's capitol. Four of the women of two generations relied on their sewing expertise to sustain themselves and their families when times were hard.

Threads of Time will touch the memories of many families who remember how hard their mothers and grandmothers worked. It's inspiring to highlight women who achieved and who touched history through their sewing.

Jeannine S. Clark
Community activist and Smithsonian Regent

Threads of Time,

The Fabric of History

Profiles of African American Dressmakers
and Designers, 1850–to the Present

By Rosemary E. Reed Miller

Washington, D.C.
2002

Inquiries should be addressed to:

Toast and Strawberries Press
1608 20th Street, NW
Washington, DC 20009

ISBN: 0–9709731–0–3
Library of Congress registration copyright: No. TX–5–383–695

Printed in the United States of America by Signature Printing, Gaithersburg, Maryland

Distributed by Toast and Strawberries Press
1608 20th Street, NW
Washington, DC 20009

Tel. (202) 234–1212
Fax (202) 723–2246
Website: toastandstrawberries.com
E-mail: Rosemaryreed4@hotmail.com

Cover Design by Kim Lyons
Book Design by Janice Sterling

pictured on the cover page:
Senator and Mrs. John F. Kennedy; sitting in chair, Anne Cole Lowe, designer of Mrs. Kennedy's wedding dress;
Back Page: Mrs. Elizabeth Keckley, author and designer for Mrs. Abraham Lincoln

Contents

Adele Alexander

Rosemary Reed's *"Threads of Time, The Fabric of History"* reveals the colorful and intricately woven dramas of African American women dressmakers. Her expertly told story moves from Mary Todd Lincoln's tempestuous personal and professional relationship with one-time slave Elizabeth Keckley, to Jackie Kennedy's cherished designer, Anne Cole Lowe, to Rosa Parks, legendary instigator of the Montgomery bus boycott—also a skilled modiste.

The women in Reed's narrative, who so effectively rose above the socially imposed limitations of race and gender, were wonderfully gifted in their craft. But more than that, they were significant players in the complex drama of United States history.

Adele Logan Alexander is professor of history at George Washington University. She is the author *"Ambiguous Lives: Free Women of Color in Rural Georgia*, 1789-1879 [1991], and *"Homelands and Waterways: The American Journey of the Bond Family,"* 1846-1926 [1999]

Acknowledgements

I want to thank all the people who have made this book a reality. Toast and Strawberries Boutique has presented a *Threads of Time* program since the 1980s. A woman who booked us to do a show in Detroit once provided me with general opening remarks about the contributions of slave dressmakers. This set me on a path to do more research and writing. The culmination of that research is the book before you today.

My friend Jerome Smith suggested the idea that people might enjoy the project as a performance or presentation during Black History Month or Women's History Month. My friend Sheila Gregory, who was doing research on a dressmaker relative, gave me the marvelous title *Threads of Time*.

I also want to thank Charlene Carmichael, who comes from a designer family as well. Her mother, Rose Batson, sold dresses to Lena Horne and to the wives of Count Basie and Perry Como. Charlene helped me with the presentations and her daughter graciously lent me the wedding dress her mother designed for her for use in our fashion shows.

People often told me about their great-aunts who were wonderful dressmakers. However, most of them did not know

MARTIN LUTHER KING, JR. LIBRARY, WASHINGTON, DC

The woman pictured from a comfortable economic background. The details of this 1870s dress show the care and skill in construction of designs nade during that period. Until the 1920's, most dresses would have 16 to 20 pieces just to make the bodice.

about the women profiled in *Threads of Time*. This strengthened my resolve to bring its material to a larger public. It is my hope that *Threads of Time: The Fabric of History* will not only bring to light the important artistic, social, and political contributions of African American women designers and dressmakers but also serve as a kind of history itself. There are, after all, many schools of life, and like many of the women profiled in the book, who learned to sew from their mothers, aunts, or grandmothers, there are many ways to pass on information to give them a place in our collective history. Women's fashion intersecting with social change and politics may surprise some readers, but the stories in this book confirm that such outcomes are truly possible and may even occur in our own time.

Over the years, many people have offered encouragement and performed the various "threads" at shows. I think especially of Zora Felton; Jeannine Clark; Nora Gregory; the late Pat Morris; Lenore Cole, who is related to Ann Cole Lowe; Diane Mance, who brought an Ann Lowe dress to one of my fashion merchandising classes at Howard University; Julie Finley, who shared memories of her Ann Lowe bridesmaid dress; Betty King, who lent the author a dress by Ann Lowe; June Bland, Ph.D., an African American textile scholar; Adele Alexander, Ph.D., for sharing her wisdom and information; Claudia Kidwell, of the Smithsonian Institution Costume section, for her work on Elizabeth Keckley; Nina Auchincloss Straight for sharing her memories of Ann Lowe; and so many others, that it is impossible to thank them all here.

We have presented the *Threads of Time: The Fabric of History* program at such places as the Smithsonian National Museum of American Art; the Women's Museum of Art; the Corcoran Art Gallery; the U.S. Departments of Energy, Housing and Urban Development, and Agriculture; Prince George's County Community College and Recreation Department; Jefferson Junior High School and Wilson High School in Washington, D.C., and for churches, sororities, and other community organizations.

I certainly had an interest in making the *Threads of Time* narrative into a book, but it was only after Director Diane Leatherman of the Friends of Montgomery County Library asked me to have a book to sell after our show that I undertook the extra research, computer training, photo searches, and oral interviews needed to produce this book.

In compiling this book, I am indebted to Lee Regan and the staff at Plymouth Public Library in Plymouth, Massachusetts, for the help that enabled me to flesh out the life of Eliza Gardner. I also wish to thank the staff at the Schlesinger Library at Radcliffe College who were helpful with New England abolitionists. Ardie Meyers of the Library of Congress African American section helped me to find a likeness of the elusive Eliza Gardner and details about her church and civic contributions. The librarians at the Martin Luther King, Jr., Library, Washingtonian section, in Washington, D.C., were immeasurably helpful providing photos and census directories. The Howard University Moorland-Spingarn Research Center suggested additional dressmakers.

The staff of Rep. John Conyers (D–Michigan) helped me reach Rosa Parks. Filmmaker Jim Byers helped me learn more about Zelda Wynn Valdes, the designer for celebrity jazz singer Joyce Bryant. Ersa Poston and Lady Sara Lou Harris shared their memories of Anne Lowe and Zelda Wynn Valdes with me. The staff at the New York Schomberg Library were helpful in pointing out sources on Wynn, as was librarian Robert Garland at the Dance Theatre of Harlem. Joyce Alexander Bailey, daughter of the founder of the Black Fashion Museum, Lois Alexander, shared her memories of her mother, the early days of National Association of Fashion and Accessory Designers, and Zelda Wynn Valdes.

I am grateful for the sensitive contribution of graphic designer Janice Sterling to the appearance of the book. I especially want to thank John M. Howard, Elaine Heffernan, Ruby M. Essien, Dora Gross, Winnie Cowgill, Paul H. Davis, Marieta Lorelle Harper, Amy Robinson, and others for help in editing the manuscript. Elaine did yeoman's work in the editing. I must, of course, express gratitude to all the designers of the past for their quiet but forceful work and to current artists and designers: Pamela Botchway, Viola Burley Leak, Saharah, Joyce Scott, Rita Johnson Falkener, Sara Penn, Frances Warren, and Cindy Williams. Special Thanks to Keith Thomas, Monica Parker and Joe Fedeli.

Above all, I want to thank my mother, Eloise S. Reed, her mother, and her great-grandmother—dressmakers and artists all—to whom I and my children Paul and Sabrina are indebted for our sense of art and style.

The selected profiles of African-American dressmakers and designers from the 1850's to the present time is a specialized and much need publication for individuals to know the struggles and challenges African-Americans endured as well as the truth of our history.

Rosemary Reed Miller has a passion for history and fashions. She has introduced a splendid fusion of historic seamstresses of African ancestry who contributed much to American history. Her entire approach was a non-stop journey through African-American history, culture and traditions. It was fascinating and has provided me an enormous appreciation of my own mother's talent in designing and sewing clothing for her three children.

This book is certain to entrall readers—because it tells the truth.

Irena L. Webster, Executive Director
The Association for the Study of African American Life and History, Inc.

Introduction

Some readers may wonder what fashion has to do with African American history. African American history is replete with distinguished and multi-talented black and white people. Many of us are familiar with celebrated names in African American history: Frederick Douglass, activist, statesman, and abolitionist; John Brown, abolitionist and insurrectionist; Booker T. Washington, educator and founder of Tuskegee Institute; Mary McLeod Bethune, renowned teacher and founder of the National Council of Negro Women; Benjamin Banneker, scholar and scientist (see reference notes); Thurgood Marshall, legal rights advocate and Supreme Court Justice; Martin Luther King, Jr., civil rights leader and recipient of the Nobel Prize for Peace; and the list goes on. Despite legal, economic and social barriers,

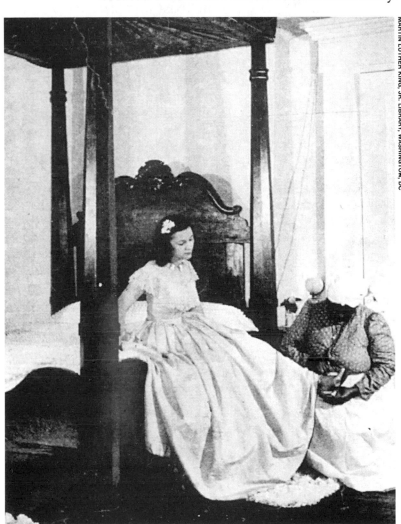

"Aunt" Lizzie Nash, family servant since birth, helps Emmaline Hardy with her slipper. Emmaline Hardy is dressing for a party at Whithall, which was built by her great-great-grandfather. Credit should be given to the family servant who designed and executed the gown that Emmaline wears.

African Americans have made great contributions to America in education, science, law, politics, music, literature, and sports. It is our hope that our research will reveal to you another field in which African Americans have excelled, a field in which we hope they will continue to contribute their talents—fashion!

This research comes to you from Toast and Strawberries, a black woman-owned business. I founded Toast in 1968. I have written this book to highlight the work of black women in dressmaking and design. This book records and illustrates the accomplishments of past design-ers and salutes their legacy to contemporary and future design-ers. As I researched this topic and conducted interviews, I was struck by how many of the women included in this study fought for justice in their com-munities and by the many peo-ple their efforts touched in the past and the present.

This group of women featured in Demorest's Magazine, *an 1840s fashion magazine, are wearing dresses typical of the period. Such magazines were passed around so that women could see what was fashionable. Women of that time gave such pictures to skilled servants to copy. In the Northern states and in the Western territories, a woman did the sewing herself or paid a dressmaker to sew the garment. In the South, slaves were expected to do the work.*

We at Toast and Strawberries hope that you will enjoy reading about women who quietly designed and made clothes for past generations. Many of these women used the income from dressmaking to invest in other fields. In addition, we are proud to introduce you to contemporary designers, some of whom have also gone on to other areas of the arts and business.

Reference Note:

Benjamin Banneker (1731–1806): A Baltimore, Maryland, African American scholar, who had very little schooling but made astronomical and weather predictions that he published in an almanac from 1792–1802. He had very few books, but he made wooden clocks and solved various mathematical problems. Banneker was also a surveyor and helped determine the boundaries of the District of Columbia.

Elizabeth Keckley dressed Mary Todd Lincoln.
She was on close terms with the Lincoln White
House. She wrote a book about her experiences,
"Thirty Years as a Slave, or Behind the Scenes."

Part I: Dressmakers of the 1850s

Elizabeth Keckley

During slavery in the United States, first in the colonies and then later in the states and territories, black women were responsible for the sewing needs of the plantation as well as the general household in the city. They mended and fashioned clothing for the mistress of the house, the family, and household servants. They also used their ingenuity and skills to make and repair the clothing of other slaves from leftover materials.

A young Lincoln.

A special talent for needlework in a black woman added to her value as a slave. Once the woman became especially competent, her time was spent producing delicate piecework for her owners. Her beautiful quilts and bedspreads were proudly displayed throughout the mansion, and her gowns were the subject of much admiration. A talented seamstress could, in her spare time, hire herself out to make dresses for the mistresses of other households. In many cases, the slave woman was able not only to hire herself out but also keep a good percentage of the money earned for her own use. One such slave was Elizabeth Keckley, who used her needlework skills to purchase her freedom. She developed such a flourishing business that she competed for and won an appointment as dressmaker for Mrs. Abraham Lincoln.

Elizabeth was born May 26, 1818, in Dinwiddie, Virginia. She was a slave of the Burwell family. When she was about eight years old, she was given to one of the Burwell daughters and her minister husband. When the couple moved to St. Louis, Elizabeth went with them. Although the family was socially upper class in St. Louis, they fell on hard times and hired Elizabeth out to sew for wealthy women in the area. Elizabeth sewed mostly evening dresses at a "market rate," which meant her prices were high. She brought in enough money from her dressmaking earnings to support seventeen people. Lizzie's only child, George, was named after her father. The man who fathered George was a friend of the Colonel's son who forced himself on Lizzie against her will. Lizzie married James Keckley in 1852 and within a few years found out he wasn't free and was an alcoholic.

By the time Mrs. Keckley was thirty years old, she had saved almost enough money to buy her freedom. Slavery was still a thriving business in 1848, and her family felt that they could increase her price because they had trained and fed Elizabeth for years. She was even more valuable because she had taught herself to read and to write. The family set the price for Mrs. Keckley and her son at $1,200. However, she still did not have the full amount, so she borrowed the sum from special customers.

Mrs. Mary Lincoln auditioned various white and black dressmakers in Washington. She chose Elizabeth Keckley,

Elizabeth could have run away—everyone felt that slavery would be ending soon anyway. One of her customers said, "Why don't you visit a friend in New York? No one ever comes back." However, Elizabeth did not want to have to run from slave bounty hunters who, authorized by the fugitive slave laws, might have chased her down and brought her back in chains. In many cases, they were known to have brought back any African American man or woman they could lay their hands on, regardless of his or her legal status as a free subject or a slave. Thus, Keckley's concerns were well founded, to say the least, but, most important, her decision was based on her desire to have a thriving, lawful business. Her decision also reflected the Nineteenth Century value of keeping a stiff upper lip, and so, with her fierce optimism, she worked hard for another year and paid off the loan. As displayed in her book, the manumission paper looks exactly like a regular contract except that it was a contract for the purchase of her freedom.

Mrs. Keckley and her son moved to Baltimore. She had letters of recommendation, but was not able to build her business to the level she had expected. She therefore moved to Washington, D.C., in early 1860. Within

who had a thriving business in Washington.

a month after her arrival, she had attracted a large clientele of wealthy ladies, including Varina Davis, wife of Jefferson Davis, who soon became President of the Confederacy.

Mrs. Davis knew that the Southern states would soon be seceding, and she asked Mrs. Keckley to join her in New Orleans, the city expected to become the capital of the newly formed Confederacy. Mrs. Keckley was tempted by the offer of guaranteed business. She knew that there were free blacks in New Orleans, but she had just purchased her freedom, and she

The White House and Washington, D.C., in the 1860s just before the Civil War.

was not sure how other Southerners would treat her. She bade Mrs. Davis a pleasant good-bye and said that she would think about the offer.

Soon after Mrs. Keckley arrived in Washington, D.C., Mrs. Lincoln started asking around for a good seamstress. She tried out several and eventually picked Keckley to do all her sewing during her four years in the White House. Keckley soon became Mrs. Lincoln's designer, her "eyes and ears" in Washington, and her traveling companion. She traveled with Mrs. Lincoln to visit her son Robert at Harvard University in Massachusetts, then to Richmond and Petersburg, Virginia, during the Civil War. They traveled to New York City and to Springfield, Illinois, after Lincoln's assasination.

Short and long capes were the general outerwear of the 1860s.

A fashionable dress of the period.

The demanding friendship with Mrs. Lincoln was a mixed blessing. It took valuable time away from Elizabeth's thriving business, but it gave her unique access to the private world of the Lincolns and occasionally provided Keckley with support for her own social and political work. Indeed, Mrs. Keckley once asked Mrs. Lincoln to donate $250 to the Contraband Relief Association, which she had founded to assist former slaves who had fled the South during the Civil War to Washington.

A profile of Mary Lincoln, who was a typical "Southern belle." She enjoyed clothes, and when she came to Washington, she felt she needed, according to Keckley, "to look better and compete with the worldly Northerners...."

Lincoln was always gracious with Ms. Keckley. After the assassination, Mrs. Lincoln gave Keckley the bloodied shirt and vest Lincoln wore that night.

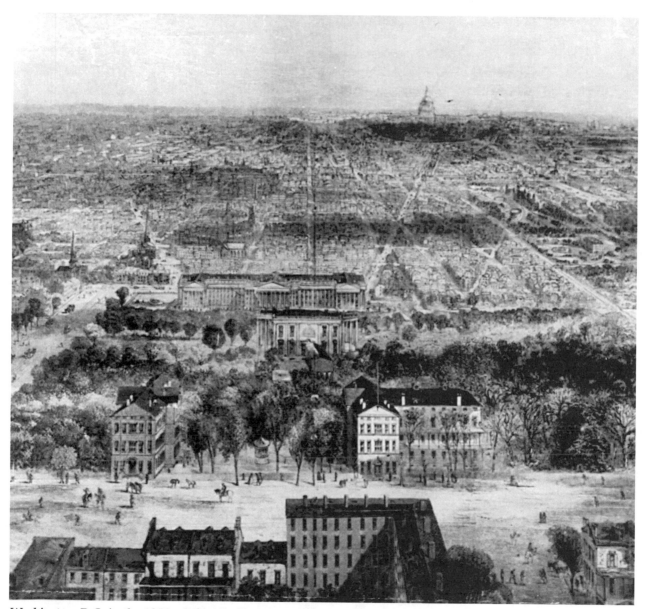

Washington, D.C. in the 1850s. When Keckley was working in Washington, it was a hot, muggy town in the summer. The muddy streets were difficult to navigate in the wet spring and winter.

Mrs. Lincoln's erratic behavior created many political and social enemies for her. Mrs. Keckley tried to explain Mrs. Lincoln to the world in her book *Thirty Years as a Slave, or Behind the Scenes*. The book provides a forthright account of the Lincoln White House and life in the 1860s in Washington. Scholars are indebted to Mrs. Keckley for her access to the Lincolns because anyone who wants an intimate perspective on the family has to refer to Keckley's book.

Although her intention was to place Mrs. Lincoln in a sympathetic light to the world, both Mrs. Lincoln and her son Robert, who was a

The Lincoln Family. Scholars are indebted to Ms. Keckley's stories about the Lincolns. No author had such long-term access to the family as did Keckley.

corporate leader at the Chicago Railroad, were offended by the publication. The publisher found it hard to distribute the book, and many black people felt that Elizabeth was a traitor to the beloved Lincolns and to the newly formed Republican Party, which, at that time, had a strong antislavery position.

As a result, Mrs. Keckley lived out her remaining forty years in obscurity. She taught school for one year at Wilberforce University in Ohio. In 1893, she represented Wilberforce College at the Columbian World's Exhibition in Chicago, Illinois, an event which celebrated the 400th Anniversary of Christopher Columbus's discovery of America. She died in 1907 in Washington at the Home for Destitute Women, a home she had assisted in establishing with earnings from her business.

Source Material

James, Edward T., *American Women Notable 1607–1950.*, et al., eds. Cambridge, Mass., Harvard University Bellnap Press, 1971.

Keckley, Elizabeth. *Thirty Years as a Slave, or Behind the Scenes*. New York: New York Times Pub. Co., 1961.

Mrs. Lincoln came to depend upon Mrs. Keckley to be her companion as well as her dressmaker.

The Gardner family lived in a rather cosmopolitan and international city, Boston, Massachusetts. Eliza Gardner was active with antislavery groups and helped find more diverse employment for young black women.

Eliza Ann Gardner

Eliza Ann Gardner, dressmaker, activist, church leader, and fundraiser for missions to the American South and to Africa, uniquely combined sewing skills with antislavery work and community service in her nine-decade life. Throughout her life, Eliza worked to free slaves in the South and to help families and women. For many years, she was a member of the African Methodist Episcopal (A.M.E.) Zion Church in Boston, Massachusetts.

There are few photos as Eliza Gardner, but one of her abolitionist correspondents was Harriet Tubman, pictured above. Tubman, freed over 300 slaves through the Underground Railway in the Maryland area. During the Civil War, she worked for the Union Army as a cook and as a spy.

Eliza was born May 28, 1831, in New York City to free parents, James and Dorothy Gardner, who earned their living by making sails for large ocean-going vessels. In 1854, the family moved to Boston, which was then the center for construction of fast clipper ships and whaling boats. They opened their business on Grove Street in the West End.

Members of the Gardner family were active in their community, and their home was a station on the Underground Railway, a system of sympathetic people and safe houses that helped fleeing slaves reach freedom in the Northern States and in Canada. (See reference notes.) Eliza attended the Boston Public School for Colored Children, the only school for blacks in Boston at that time. She was fortunate to have parents who wanted to educate her and could afford to do so. Eliza was a brilliant student and won many scholarships and awards. She parlayed the family sewing tradition into dressmaking and general fine needlework. She was quite organized in her business and did well. For example, she secured the contract to make the banner for the Odd Fellows Lodge in Plymouth, Massachusetts.

Ms. Gardner was recognized as a highly skilled seamstress. She was called a "mantua maker." "Mantua" is an old Italian word referring to skill in detail work. Mantua makers were valued for their expertise in making the large hoop skirts and intricate bodices fashionable in those times.

Wendell Phillips was a fiery antislavery orator. He joined William Lloyd Garrison as a member of the American Anti-Slavery Society. He joined Charles Sumner in working for the passage of the Fifteenth Amendment, which gave freed male slaves the vote. The amendment was passed in 1870.

Eliza Gardner worked to place young black women in jobs traditionally held by whites. Her efforts in the 1850s to help train and then place black women in new job areas were later formalized by groups such as the National Urban League. (See reference notes.)

Because of her lecturing and activism in the 1850s, Eliza Gardner became known as the "Julia Ward Howe of the Negro race." Julia Ward Howe, writer, reformer, women's voting rights activist, and founder of Mother's Day, wrote the poem "The Battle Hymn of the Republic." Later, the poem was set to an old folk tune. The words "I have seen John Brown's body a-mould'ring in the grave" became part of the unofficial anthem of the Union Army during the Civil War. (See reference notes.)

Ms. Gardner's independent spirit brought her into contact with antislavery leaders such as William Lloyd Garrison, Senator Charles Sumner, black abolitionist Lewis Hayden, Frederick Douglass, Harriet Tubman, and Sojourner Truth. Gardner once shared a platform with Douglass and Sumner. (See reference notes.)

In *The African Methodist Episcopal Zion Church: Reality of the Black Church* (1974), William Jacob Walls reports that Ms. Gardner proudly told him that she was a blood relative of writer and activist W. E. B. DuBois. David Levering Lewis states in his biography of Dubois that Gardner knew DuBois during and after his Harvard years and that she proudly introduced the historian to the Rev. J. C. Price, founder of Livingstone College in Salisbury, North Carolina. "Throughout most of her life," wrote Sierra and Jones in *Notable Black American Women, Book II*, "Gardner was a member of the African Methodist Episcopal (A.M.E.) Zion Church in Boston. As a religious leader, she was known in the denomination as the 'Mother' of

Charles Sumner was a U.S. senator who worked tirelessly to see that freed slaves could vote and have basic civil rights. His insistence that former slaves needed as many rights as possible to participate as citizens was visionary for that time.

the A.M.E. Zion Missionary Society, which raised money for missionaries to the American South and to Africa. She also served as the vice-president of the Missionary Society's New England Conference." In 1865, according to *Notable Black American Women, Book II,* "when the Columbus Avenue Church in Boston began a drive to purchase a larger facility, Gardner and her mother became founding contributing members. At this time, she launched a lifetime career of teaching Sunday school. In 1883, she became the first Sunday School superintendent for Boston, (and the only one to do so until 1918)." She was an officer and fundraiser with the Ladies' Home and Foreign Missionary Society of the A.M.E. Zion Church. The group raised over a thousand dollars to send missionaries to the South and Andrew Cartwright and his family to Liberia and West Africa in 1876.

In 1884, in North Carolina, the prominent role of women in raising missionary funds came under fire by male ministers. Gardner listened quietly and finally spoke bravely in defense of the women's work (*A.M.E. Zion Quarterly Review,* January 1894, p. 500): "I come from old Massachusetts, where we have declared that all, not only men, but women, too, are created free and equal. . . my brethren here will regard this as rank heresy. . . . Not only this heresy (equality), but temperance reform, the antislavery cause, and many other good movements had their birth in the old Bay State. . . if I would go back to Boston and tell the people that some of the members of this Conference were against the women, it might have a tendency to preju- dice our interests in that city with those whom we can rely [on] for [money] assistance. . . . [I]f you commence to talk about the superiority of men . . . we cannot help you in New England one bit." Under Gardner's direction, the A.M.E. Zion Church New England Conference Missionary Society raised almost half of the monies used for missionary and church building work.

In 1893, Gardner's social activism took a new turn when she became a founder of the Women's Era Club of Boston. Later, in 1895, she served as chaplain of the National Federation of Afro-American Women, which later merged with the National Association of Colored Women. In the 1908 bien- nial convention of the organization, the seventy-seven-year-old Gardner was featured as an honored guest.

By the 1850s, Boston was relatively well developed and was a destination and a stop for fleeing slaves.

Threads of Time   *19*

In 1909, Gardner founded the Butler Club of the Boston A.M.E. Zion Church, which was named for one of the original members of the church. She continued to be active in the church, principally as a fundraiser for missionary work. She had discontinued her sewing business, but, in 1916, she presented quite a handsome quilt that was auctioned to raise money. She remained president of the Butler Club until her death in Boston on January 4, 1922, at age ninety-one.

Source Material

William Jacob Walls. *The African Methodist Episcopal Zion Church: Reality of the Black Church.* Charlotte, NC: A.M.E. Zion Publishing House, 1974.

Notable Black American Women, Book II, ed. Jessie Carney Smith.

Gale Research. Excerpts from National Association of Colored Women, 1978.

Hallie Quinn Brown and Sarah Fleming. *Homespun Heroines and Other Women of Distinction.* Xenia, Ohio: Aldine Publishing, 1926.

David Levering Lewis. *W.E.B. DuBois: Biography of a Race, 1868–1919.* New York: Henry Holt, 1993.

Howard University Spingarn-Moorland Research Center, research staff.

Kathy Herrlich, Radcliffe College Schlesinger Library, Boston, Massachusetts.

Plymouth Public Library: Herman Hunt volunteers, History Room; Beverly Ness, Reference associate; and Lee Regan, Adult Services.

Library of Congress: Ms. Artie Meyers, African American Section; Research Facility.

Reference Notes

Underground Railroad (1800–1863): The route(s) used by antislavery supporters to help slaves escape from the South to either free Northern states or to Canada before Emancipation in 1863 until the end of the Civil War. The Railroad's "stations" were homes and barns that provided safe passage on the "rails." The "rails" went through Ohio to central Canada, or through Maryland and on to Maine and eastern Canada. Even though the Fugitive Slave Act was passed in 1793, people were still actively protecting fleeing slaves during the 1840s and 1850s. Many slaves would either stay in the North or return from Canada to help bring up their remaining kin.

Julia Ward Howe's activism extended to education and prison reform, abolition of slavery, and the establishment of a day of recognition for mothers.

Urban League (*started in 1910*): The Urban League is an organization that was founded to secure African Americans economic self-reliance, parity, civil rights, and political power. It is a community-based organization with professionally-staffed affiliate offices in over a hundred cities in thirty-four states and the District of Columbia. The Urban League has worked with other civil rights groups, such as the National Association for the Advancement of Colored People (NAACP), to ensure that African Americans obtain skills through education, have opportunity to work in a wide range of jobs, and pursue happiness in the same manner as other Americans.

Julia Ward Howe (1819–1910): A writer, lecturer, and social reformer, Julia Ward Howe is remembered today for her poem "The Battle Hymn of the Republic," which was later put to music and became the marching song of the Union Army during the Civil War. The lines "John Brown [the antislavery activist] lies a-mould'ring in the grave. His soul goes marching on..." was an inspiration for the "We Shall Overcome" song of the civil rights movement in the 1960s, a century later. Howe was born in New York City of wealthy parents. She married another reformer-activist, Samuel Gridley Howe. Both worked for prison, educational, and deaf reform. Both wrote for the *Commonwealth*, an abolitionist newspaper. After the Civil War, Julia Howe worked for feminist groups and the vote for women, part of an effort that did not succeed until 1920, two years after her death. Howe traveled around the world, and her daughters continued her work in literature and in social reform.

Frederick Douglass (1817?–1895): Douglass was born into slavery near Easton, Maryland. He was hired out to work on the docks in Baltimore. There, he realized he could flee via a ship to Boston. After reaching Massachusetts, he became active in the antislavery movement. He spoke to groups all over the U. S. and for two years in the British Isles. He went on to found the *North Star,* an abolitionist newspaper. He also wrote *The Narrative of the Life of Frederick Douglass,* an account of his life under slavery. Douglass discussed the problems of slavery with President Lincoln and organized two colored regiments to fight in the Civil War. He received many honors during his life. He was appointed Ambassador to Haiti (1889–91) and Recorder of Deeds for the District of Columbia. He died in his beautiful mansion on a hill in Anacostia in southeast, D.C. His home is maintained by the U. S. Park Service and is open to the public.

A young Frederick Douglass. Abolitionist, orator, statesman.

John Brown (1800–1859): John Brown was an ardent abolitionist. Not only did he and his followers abhor slavery but they also felt they could actually lead an uprising of slaves in a war against slavery. In "The Battle Hymn of the Republic," Julia Ward Howe pays homage to him: "John Brown's body lies a-mould'ring in the grave. His soul goes marching on." Brown was born in Torrington, Connecticut, to a family that had come to America in the 1700s, during the colonial period. He worked and farmed in various parts of the country, marrying twice, but hardly earning a living off marginal farmland to support his large family. He arrived in Kansas in 1855, right after the Kansas-Nebraska Bill that allowed residents the choice of a slave or free territory. There was fierce fighting among the Missouri and Kansas settlers, but the effort to make Kansas a "free" state failed. In 1859, Brown with twenty followers planned to take over the Army arsenal at Harper's Ferry, West Virginia. The take-over was a stalemate until they were routed by the Army led by Colonel Robert E. Lee. Brown and the few followers who survived the battle were hanged in 1859. The passage of the Fugitive Slave Law, the publication of Uncle Tom's Cabin, which further exposed the misery of slavery, the 1857 Dred Scott decision, which sent captured slaves back to their owners, and the battle at Harper's Ferry, all inflamed public opinion, either proslavery or antislavery, and set the country on the path to the Civil War.

Harriet Tubman (c.1823–1913): Numerous historians place Tubman's birthplace in Dorchester County, Maryland. She wrote that as a young girl, she did heavy labor year in and year out as a field hand. In 1849, she escaped to free territory in the North, and there she decided to help other slaves escape from their backbreaking bondage. She guided over three hundred people—men, women, and children— through the Underground Railway. Tubman risked her life on every journey. If she were caught by slave bounty hunters, she would lose her own hard won freedom. She was called "Moses" after the biblical Moses who led the Israelites out of bondage in Egypt. During the Civil War, 1861–65, Tubman worked as a cook, scout, and spy for the Union Army. After the Civil War, she saw the need for newly freed slaves to be educated. Accordingly, she worked to set up schools in North Carolina.

Sojourner Truth (1797–1883): Facts about Sojourner Truth's early life are sketchy. She was born in 1797, daughter of James and Elizabeth Baumfree, slaves of a Dutch farmer in Hurley, Ulster County in New York State. Her first language was Dutch. Sojourner, at 11 years old, was separated from her mother, who gave her the very religious focus she held to all of her life.

She endured 30 years of slavery. She became free in 1827 under the Emancipation Act of New York State.

In 1843, when she was 46 years old, she assumed the name "Truth" for God, and "Sojourner" because she was to "travel up and down the land" testifying. She became aligned with the Feminist movement, and became an Abolitionist—to abolish slavery. She worked with William Lloyd Garrison, who believed in equality of the sexes, and the publisher of the fiery newspaper, the "Liberator," Wendell Phillips, the grand orator, Frederick Douglass, the black statesmen, and other Abolitionists.

Sojourner Truth

Sojourner was described as being almost six feet tall, a spellbinding orator, very dark skin, with a deep bass voice, and a remarkable singer. She traveled to conferences in the Midwest and Middle Atlantic States. In Indiana, her critics openly claimed she was a man. At one rally, Ms. Truth scandalized the audience and her critics by opening her shirt and asked them to look. She also gave her famous speech, "Ain't I a woman too?" in which she reminded her audience that she had borne children, and had also worked hard all her life. She moved to Battle Creek, Michigan, where she died at the age of 86 in 1883.

From notes in *Black Women in Sisterhood in Action,* Feb. 1986 Newsletter.

Lewis Hayden (1815–1889): Lewis Hayden was a runaway slave from Kentucky, who made his way to Boston, founded a tailoring business, became active in the white and black communities, opened his home to other fugitive slaves as a station in the Underground Railroad, and was appointed in 1859 to be messenger to the Massachusetts Secretary of State (probably one of the the only Negro office holders before the Civil War, later in 1873, elected to the State Legislature).

Hayden, and his family were helped to escape by the assistance of the Rev. Calvin Fairbanks and Miss Delia A. Webster. Both were imprisoned, Miss Webster for a few months, Fairbanks for 10 years. Finally, Heyden raised $650 as a ransom to free Fairbanks.

Reference

Articles, Schlesinger Library

COURTESY OF SHEILA GREGORY THOMAS

Margaret Hagan, entrepreneur, right, with sister.
She used her sewing skills as a stepping stone for
business development.

Margaret Hagan

We are lucky that Elizabeth Keckley, dressmaker for Mrs. Lincoln, wrote a book about her life in *Thirty Years as A Slave, Or Behind the Scenes.* Information about early dressmakers often comes to us from oral family history. In researching their family history, the Gregory family of Washington, D.C., found two interesting items: not only did they have a wealthy great-great-great-grandfather, Po Mohammitt, from the island of Madagascar, 250 miles off the east coast of Africa, but they also had an entrepreneur-dressmaker in their family. The entrepreneur-dressmaker was Margaret Mohammit Hagan, daughter of Janey and Po Mohammit.

Po Mohammit, according to oral tradition and documented by the Gregory family, descended from the family of a Sultan in central Madagascar. Po Mohammit came to the Frederick, Maryland area around 1800. He met and fell in love with a woman named "Janey" who worked in the Roger Brooke Taney household. Tradition, but not documents, affirm that Janey was the daughter of owner Taney, who was also the Chief Justice of the Supreme Court. Justice Taney's decision in the 1840s against the slave Dred Scott, who sued for his freedom because he had lived in a "free state" incensed anti-slavery supporters. (See reference notes).

Po Mohammit paid $1,400 for the lovely Janey. Most slaves sold for $200 to $600. However, if they were educated, skilled, or attractive, the price would go higher. The family understood that Po wanted Janey for a wife, was well traveled and seemed to have

Washington in the 1890s, about the time when Margaret was prospering in the dressmaker business.

financial assets. The Taneys charged accordingly. The couple married and purchased property. Mohammit raised racehorses and prospered. Among the children born to them was Margaret Mohammit Hagen, the subject of this profile.

Life as a free person of color in the South was often difficult and became more so with the approach of the Civil War. So, in 1861, Margaret Hagan decided to sell her home in Maryland and go to Philadelphia. She tells the story of bounty hunters who boarded the train she was traveling on, forcing her to hide under the skirts of a sympathetic white woman to avoid capture.

In the late 1800s, after living for many years in Pennsylvania, where she owned a laundry, Hagan moved to Washington, D.C., and established a dressmaking business. She advertised her services in a local directory to attract women customers to her shop. In these ads, she invited potential clients to come and see her dressmakers' magic scale. Margaret had a small staff and a well-run business.

However, being a dressmaker was not Hagan's ultimate goal. She planned to use dressmaking as a stepping-stone to her real objective for living in the nation's capital: the study of medical electricity. She studied in both Philadelphia and Washington to learn the use of electricity for improving a person's health. On becoming certified as a practitioner of medical electricity, she set up business in Williamsport, Pennsylvania, where she catered to a wealthy clientele that included bankers and lumbermen. By the time she was eighty, Margaret Hagan had owned and operated three such establishments, two in Pennsylvania and one in New Jersey.

When she was in her eighties, Hagan joined her daughter Fannie, who was married to Professor James Monroe Gregory. Gregory was head of Bordentown Training School in New Jersey. There, Margaret opened a sanitarium—what we would today call a health spa—which soon became a favorite of the leading citizens of Bordentown. She managed the sanitarium successfully, but she became so intrusive in the affairs of the

Roger B. Taney, slave owner and second United States Supreme Court Justice, who ruled in 1857 against the freedom plea from slave Dred Scott.

Haffner Daniel, butcher, 45 F ne
Haffner Henry C, salesman, 804 K nw
Haffner Christian, driver, 1404 H ne
Hagan Cornelia J, clk treas, The Lexington
**Hagan Edward H, dumb waiters,
910 11th nw**

preme court D C, 1818 H nw
**Hagner Charles E, physician, 1400
H nw**

Office Hours: {8:30 to 9:30 a m
{12 to 1 p m
{6 to 7 p m

MRS. MARGARET A. HAGAN,

Is stopping for a short time at

1109 F STREET, NW.,   WASHINGTON, D. C.

Where she cordially invites the Ladies to call and investigate the

Dressmakers' Magic Scale.

Advertisement in Gazette newspaper in 1870s. Hagen's business was located at 1109 F St, NW. She had 4 to 33 employees, and ran an organized business sewing for comfortably-situated women in downtown Washington.

WASHINGTON ARCHITECTURE.

Modest dwellings of African Americans in Washington, D.C. in the 1880s.

Bordentown School, that the family had her committed to an institution. Today, we would probably recognize her condition as dementia.

Professor Gregory, an Oberlin College graduate, went on to become one of the first three instructors at Howard University, which was started after the Civil War by Colonel Otis Howard who was concerned about educating freed slaves. The Gregory family has had generations of achievers in America—scholars, activists, lawyers, artists, and government officials. Frederick Gregory, for instance, a Washington, D.C., native, was an astronaut, and the first black to pilot a space shuttle.

Mrs. Hagan died in New Jersey in the mid-1900s and was buried in Baltimore, Maryland.

Reference Notes

Roger Brooke Taney (1777–1864): Taney is mostly remembered as the Chief Justice of the Supreme Court who tried to weaken the Federal Bank system and ruled against the slave Dred Scott in a celebrated Supreme Court case. The decision against Dred Scott intensified the division between North and South and accelerated the events that brought on the Civil War. Taney was born in Calvert County, Maryland, went to Dickinson College, and was admitted to the bar in 1799. He later moved to Frederick, Maryland and became a leading lawyer and political figure. He became a state senator.

President Andrew Jackson appointed him U. S. Attorney General. In 1833, Taney became Secretary of the Treasury. He angered Congress by withdrawing deposits from the Central Treasury. He retired, but in 1836, Jackson appointed him Chief Justice of the Supreme Court. Taney favored states' rights, which led him to rule against Dred Scott.

Dred Scott: A slave of army surgeon John Emerson of Missouri. Emerson first took Scott with him to the "free state" of Illinois, then to the Minnesota Territory, a state that was precluded from becoming a slave state by the Missouri Compromise of 1820, which tried to balance territories coming into the federation between "slave" or "free" States. In 1838, Emerson took Scott back to Missouri and sold him to another owner.

Scott sued for his freedom on the basis that his residence was in a free territory state. The case reached the U. S. Supreme Court, which was heard by Roger Brooke Taney. Taney ruled that Scott was still a slave, because he did not have the rights of a citizen, that he was actually in a "slave" state, that is, Missouri, and that the Missouri Compromise was not legally binding. When the ruling was read, riots ensued. John Brown later failed in his attempt to take over the federal arms cache at Harper's Ferry, West Virginia. Tensions flared, and the Civil War was declared soon thereafter.

Source Material

Information obtained from Sheila Gregory Thomas. Oral Family History Project of the Gregory Family, Washington, DC, 2002.

MARTIN LUTHER KING, JR. LIBRARY, WASHINGTON, DC

Washington, D.C. in the 1890s. On the lower right, African Americans selling at the market. Washington was the first stop for fleeing slaves. Many stayed on to establish thriving businesses: hotels, liveries, restaurants, and contractors.

Ann Lowe in her trademark black hat and dress.
In her later years, she had failing eyesight.

Part II: Designers of the 1950s

Ann Cole Lowe

Ann Cole Lowe was born in 1898, in Clayton County, Alabama. The social elite in New York, the Biddles, Vanderbilts, and Rockefellers wore her exquisite designs, but her lasting fame lies in the most photographed dress of its time—the wedding dress she designed for Jacqueline Bouvier.

Ann Lowe was the grandchild of a slave woman named "Georgia" and a free black man, General Cole. The couple moved to Montgomery, Alabama, where their daughter Jane later sewed for wealthy women in town. Ann helped her mother with the sewing. When Ann was sixteen, her mother died. Although coping with grief, Ann had to finish four unfinished gowns for Emmett O'Neal, wife of the governor of Alabama.

Ann Lowe's life had wonderful ups and downs. She married a black man named Lee Cohen. The marriage did not work, but it produced a son, Arthur Cohen, who handled her business until his untimely death in a car accident in 1958.

In 1915, she obtained a sewing position with a wealthy lady, D.C. Lee, of Tampa,

COURTESY OF LOIS ALEXANDER

Ann Lowe not only made lovely dresses but also skillfully sketched her designs. Her dresses were meant to evoke a "grand entrance" feeling. No two of her dresses were alike. She cut a swatch of material with the sketch and filed it so it would not be repeated.

Anne Lowe used only the finest of materials to make her dresses. Most designs carried her signature flower motif. She used her memory of real life flowers to inspire her. (Courtesy of Black Fashion Museum, NYC, 1987)

Florida, who invited Ann to come to Florida to make the gowns for her daughter's wedding party. From 1915 to 1928, Ann lived and worked in Tampa, except for a year during 1916–17, when she attended the S.L. Taylor School of Design in New York City. Ann told her relatives that the year in New York was a lonely, difficult time. She was the only black person in the school, and school officials placed her in a room apart from the other students.

However, in 1919, when she was twenty-one, she married a second time and opened her first shop, "Annie Cohen's Designs." The marriage did not work, but the shop prospered. She sadly joked to friends that her husband wanted "a real wife, not someone who was forever jumping out of bed to sketch."

By 1928, Ann, who was now calling herself "Ann Lowe," had saved $19,000, which she used to open a third-floor loft on Lexington Avenue in New York City. It took a few years before the name "Ann Lowe" became synonymous with fine gowns and eveningwear. Part of what distinguished her from her peers was that Lowe never did the same design twice. She became known for her delicate handwork and her special signature flowers. Lowe also excelled in the use of "trapunto," a tech-

A close up of the Jackie Kennedy wedding dress.

nique whereby the fabric is raised with stitching around the sides to create a three-dimensional effect. She always tried to find the best silks and to construct each dress so well that it made the wearer look her best.

She is appropriately called the "Dean of American Designers." She spent over fifty years creating fashions for the nation's leading families. According to writer Thomas B. Congdon, in a 1966 issue of the Saturday Evening Post, "Rich women pass[ed] her name among themselves; some even had her designs copied; some even cheated her." Although it is perhaps ironic that Congdon entitled his article, "Ann Lowe: Society's Best-Kept Secret," it is nevertheless true that as both an African American woman designer as well as a dressmaker for the rich and famous, this notable "Dean of American Designers" has perhaps never been as well known as her most famous dress or clients.

In 1965, Ann opened a shop on Madison Avenue, a prestigious address for any business. Indeed, today Calvin Klein has an operation on the second floor of this location. As Ann Lowe herself once stated, "I'm particular about whom I sew for. I love my clothes and I'm an awful snob. I'm not interested in sewing for café society or for social climbers." On her walls, there were pictures of the

Cleveland debutante, Betty King, of the White Sewing Machine family, flew to New York for her Ann Lowe Dress.

Duponts, the Lodges, and the Roosevelts. She was a designer who picked her clients carefully.

Betty King, who lives in Florida and Washington, D.C., remembers flying from her hometown of Cleveland to be fitted for her debutante dress. She does not know how her mother or stockbroker father heard of Lowe, but she joined other debutantes who were being presented in other cities who knew about Ann Lowe.

Betty King pictured at her debutante party. Ann Lowe designed over 2,000 wedding and coming out dresses in the 1950–60s.

Lowe also designed for wealthy black women and her family in Alabama. Her niece, Dr. Lenore Cole Alexander, who headed the Department of Labor Women's Bureau, remembers being sent fabric to practice on to continue the Cole sewing tradition. Dr. Cole also recalled that in 1953, Janet (Mrs. Hugh D. Auchincloss) asked Ann to design the wedding dress and bridal party gowns for the marriage of her daughter, Jacqueline Bouvier, to Senator John F. Kennedy. Jan Pottker, in her book, *Jackie and Janet*, wrote that Jackie had wanted a simple design, but Joe Kennedy wanted a more traditional dress. Also, the politically ambitious father was quite pleased to learn that the designer, Ann Lowe, was a 'colored' woman. The wedding gown was one of the most photographed dresses in history. The media loved Jackie and John, and almost every paper in the world ran the picture.

Ann's roller coaster life continued. What she expected to be a job with a $700 profit was wiped out one week before the wedding. Water pipes broke in the shop, and ten of the sixteen gowns were ruined. Ann had to repurchase fabric and have her staff work night and day to finish the gowns. She suffered a $2,000 loss.

Lenore Cole continues the story: "Ann personally delivered the gowns to the famous Hyannisport estate. When she arrived at the front door, the butler told her that she would have to enter through the back tradesmen's door. "My Aunt's response was: 'If I have to enter by the back door, the bride and bridesmaids would not be dressed for the wedding.' She was immediately admitted through the front door!"

Barbara Hunter, a home economics teacher at Wilson High School in Washington, D.C., met Ms. Lowe when she was a design student in New York. "It was the 1960s, and by that time she was having trouble with her eyesight—dictating her designs to her staff. She was frail, but feisty. The clothes I saw were works of art."

Five of Lowe's gowns are in the New York City Metropolitan Museum of Art—a tribute to her enduring artistic talent. Washington's Black Fashion Museum has a small collection too.

Ann Lowe died in 1981. She had treasured memories of her trips to Paris and friendships with such people as Christian Dior and Marjorie Merriweather Post who introduced her as "the head of the American House of Ann Lowe" to Dior.

Source Material

> Congdon, Thomas B. "Ann Lowe: Society's Best-Kept Secret," *Saturday Evening Post,* 1966.
> Personal Interviews with Betty King, Lenore Cole, and Barbara Hunter, 2001.

Jack and Jackie pose for pictures after their wedding.

Partial view of the large wedding party. In front are pictured sisters, Nina Auchincloss Straight, Lee, and sister-in law, Ethel Kennedy.

Political activists Septima Clark and Rosa Parks exchange ideas at the Highland Folk School, 1955.

COURTESY OF ROSA PARKS

Rosa McCauley Parks

Rosa McCauley Parks was born in Tuskegee, Alabama, in 1913 to a teacher and a carpenter. She was one of two children. Her refusal to give up her seat on a bus set off a struggle that is remembered as the "Civil Rights Movement." Andrew Young, former ambassador to the United Nations, congressman, and mayor of Atlanta, Georgia, observed: "Her action started the bus boycott that changed segregation law."

Rosa learned sewing from her grandmother and secretarial skills at the Montgomery Industrial School for Girls. In 1932, she married Raymond Parks who was secretly active in the National Association for the Advancement of Colored People, or NAACP. Rosa, inspired by Raymond's activism, became one of two women in Montgomery brave enough to join the NAACP in the 1940s.

The NAACP was founded in 1906 to fight racial discrimination in America. African Americans had won rights to citizenship and the vote with the passage of the Fourteenth and Fifteenth Amendments to the U.S.

Twelfth Street in Detroit, 1975, was named 'Rosa Parks Boulevard.'

Martin Luther King, Jr. was drawn into leadership during the Montgomery Bus Boycott

Constitution, but in the 1890s, many Southern states enacted ordinances and decrees to separate African Americans from whites in public facilities, including drinking fountains, taxis, schools, and public transportation. The laws and practice of racial segregation were called "Jim Crow."

All over the U. S., African Americans protested such laws, but hate groups, such as the Ku Klux Klan, created a climate of fear by shooting and lynching people who publicly resisted. Eventually, massive protests began to affect public and legal sentiment. Mary Ellen Pleasant, for example, successfully sued the San Francisco Trolley Company, and everyone was allowed to sit anywhere on trolleys. In Washington, D.C., streetcars were desegregated, thanks to activist Sojourner Truth who complained and won a suit against a rude conductor in 1865.

Blacks in the South and throughout the United States faced discrimination in public, tax-funded buildings, housing, and in transportation.

Rosa Parks was quiet and middle class. She was also active with the NAACP. They felt she would be the 'perfect' choice for challenging the bus company's demeaning rules which required blacks to give up their seats so that whites would never have to stand while a black sat.

Ms. Parks being finger printed in Montgomery, Alabama. She was fined $14 for disobeying municipal laws.

Mrs. Parks rode the bus every day to her job at the Montgomery Fair Department Store where she did alterations as a seamstress. On the evening of December 1, 1955, three African Americans gave up their seats to whites entering the bus and then stood in the rear of the bus, but Rosa Parks, who was sitting in the middle of the bus, refused to give up her seat. She was taken to the courthouse jail, where she was released on bail and told to return the following Monday to pay a $14.00 fine.

E. D. Nixon, head of the Montgomery, Alabama NAACP, Fred Gray, an activist lawyer, and Jo Ann Robinson, of the Women's Political Council at Alabama State College, had been looking for a suitable defendant in a test case against the bus line for months. When they heard about Rosa's refusal, they immediately formed the Montgomery Improvement Association (MIA), with ministers Ralph Abernathy and Martin Luther King, Jr., as their spokespersons. MIA held a public meeting at the Dexter Avenue Baptist Church that drew a crowd of over four thousand irate people. Flyers that night told about Rosa, and said:

DON'T RIDE THE BUS MONDAY!!!

On Monday, December 5, when Mrs. Parks and the MIA went to court to appeal the fine, few people were riding the buses.

Newspapers from all over the world covered the "Walking City" that Montgomery had become. People pooled rides in cars, taxies, and walked. Eventually, a fleet of 380 cars transported over thirty thousand people daily until the Supreme Court ruled in support of MIA. On November 20, 1956, the Court declared that the bus system's sitting ordinance was unconstitutional. The bus company finally relented and complied with the ruling, and on December 20, 1956, the boycott ended.

Mrs. Parks lost her job after her employers heard about her arrest, and her husband was harassed on his job as a barber. They decided to join her mother and brother in Detroit, Michigan, where they found it easier to earn a living. Rosa continued to work as a seamstress and joined the Board of the NAACP. In 1956, she joined the staff of Michigan Rep. John Conyers to work with constituents. She is now retired.

After the boycott, Rosa moved to Detroit, Michigan, where she worked for Congressman John Conyers, pictured above.

Although Mrs. Parks's husband and partner in her civil rights work died in 1976, she continues to speak to groups around the country and to receive numerous awards. In Montgomery, there is a street named in her honor. Rosa Parks won the NAACP Spingarn Medal in 1979 and the Martin Luther King, Jr., Nonviolent Peace Prize in 1980. She used a Roger Joseph Prize of $10,000 to fund the Raymond and Rosa Parks Self-Development Institute for Educational Work with Young People.

Because of the courageous stand taken by this quiet, but proud seamstress, demeaning racial customs in the South and the nation were forever changed. Although it is not commonly known that the woman who sparked the famous Montgomery Bus Boycott was a seamstress, it is part of the larger project of this book to link together the often little known facts of history with the larger historical events with which more of us are familiar. The actions of Rosa Parks remind us that grand words, like "history" and "politics," are made possible by the contributions not just of presidents and heads of states, but also by the actions of ordinary people who are willing to lend a hand to make or alter the "fabric of history," if you will, and thereby stitch together a sturdy fabric of community and social resistance that is historically and politically consequential.

For indeed, the Montgomery Bus Boycott sparked the organization of the Southern Christian Leadership Conference (SCLC) and the Student Nonviolent Coordinating Committee (SNCC). Both organizations challenged segregation in public accommodations and violations of voting rights throughout the U.S. The civil rights workers ultimately inspired other oppressed peoples around the world to fight for their rights

Source Material

Parks, Rosa. *My Story Dial Publishing, 1990.*.

Frances Warren—
Designer, and union activist

Willie Frances Warren

Willie Frances Warren, a dressmaker and designer in Newport News, Virginia, has a story different from those of other designers I have profiled. She not only worked out of her home doing designs for relatives and friends, but also worked in a garment factory producing children's clothes and was active in the International Ladies Garment Workers Union (ILGWU).

COURTESY OF GWEN NIX

Clown outfit designed by Frances Warren for Bernadette Harris Brooks, 1970s

Other dressmakers were active in trade organizations, such as the National Association of Fashion and Accessory Designers (NAFAD), but unionism, organizing for better pay and working conditions, was critical to the safety and progress of working dressmakers the world over. Women in many parts of the world have been the major clothing makers, usually for and inside the home, but taking those skills outside of the home has been critical to the household income of many families. However, finding a safe and well-paying position was often difficult. In New England and in New York City, the heart of the garment industry, there were sweatshops with crowded conditions and actual accidents and fires which resulted in injuries and in death of women from the 1890s to the 1930s.

Frances Warren, was born in 1926. She worked for the Gloria Manufacturing Company for just under five years. The Gloria Company had moved from New York City to Newport News, Virginia, and had contracts to work on children's clothes. Women worked on the overlock machine, which trims and sews two seams in an overlocking pattern so that the edges are finished, sturdy, and difficult to separate when worn. Frances recalled, "We used an overlock machine. It had four spools of thread, with two needles and complicated threading to produce a strong, finished edge and seams. We had a quota for the week. It wasn't hard, and you usually could make the quota, or exceed it. In 1975, with overtime, we were able to bring home over $300 a month. The pay wouldn't make you rich, but as a woman, you could use your sewing skills to supplement the family income." Frances set in sleeves and did the finishing or "closed" the garments, which were mostly pants outfits. Frances not only sewed for the garment factory but was also elected treasurer of the Virginia State AFL-CIO, which, in 1976, had almost three hundred members. Her Local 563, a branch of the ILGWU, represented the sewers at Gloria Manufacturing.

COURTESY OF FRANCES WARREN

Pictured above is mother of Frances Warren, Annie Bell Tobias, wearing a dress designed by Warren. Frances Warren and her sister, Viola Plenty, were both active in the International Garment Workers' Union in Norfolk, Virginia.

The ILGWU was formed in 1900 through the amalgamation of seven local unions in the New York area. It represented mostly immigrant workers who had been exploited over the years by long hours and appalling working conditions. After 1940, and under the presidency of David Dubinsky, the ILGWU gained the respect of manufacturers by its willingness to assist employees and employers in the industry with loans and technical assistance. There were over three hundred thousand members in the 1940s. Over the years, however, membership shrank as a result of cheap imports and transfer of factories overseas. In 1995, the remaining ILGWU membership of 125,000 merged with the 170,00-member Amalgamated Clothing and Textile Workers Union to form the Union of Needletrades, Industrial and Textile Employees (UNITE).

Frances Warren worked in a clothing industry that was migrating to the South in order to compete with import clothing. Lower cost Southern labor worked for several years, but, as more and more trade barriers and tariffs fell, lower-cost imports increased. Garment factories left the United States for the special incentives offered by developing countries. The Gloria Manufacturing Company responded to pricing pressures by moving to Newport News, Virginia from New York City. The company had contracts for Bonjour jeans, bell-bottom pants, and did work for Sears & Roebuck.

COURTESY OF WARREN FAMILY

At the height of its business, the Gloria factory employed almost three hundred people. At first, most of the seamstresses were African Americans, but, later, Caucasians and Asians were employed. The Asian employees were resettling in that area, and they had traditional sewing skills. Frances's sister, Viola Plenty, also worked for the company and was elected president of ILGWU Local 563. However, business began to slow in the late 1960s, and the factory closed in 1978. "I read articles in the local papers, the Times Herald, and the Daily Press, that the factory was slowing. It was a large employer in the area, and we were all worried," Frances remembered.

Mrs. Warren designed this wedding dress for Bernadette Harris Brooks in the 1970s.

The needle trades still exist in New York, in the South, and California, but in much reduced numbers from the 1920s–50s. Frances Warren's story is indicative of that trend.

Frances had sewn for family, friends, and a few outside customers before working in the factory. After the factory closed, she continued with her own sewing business. She designed mostly wedding and special occasion outfits. She designed her sister Bernadette's wedding dress. Her daughter Teresa also used the dress, which was a very light blue satin, fitted at the waist, with a long, flared skirt. It had a very narrow choker collar, a back zipper, and lace caps covering the shoulders and back. The details of the dress and color make it a prime example of Frances Warren's design and sewing skills.

She has also designed traditional dresses for first communions, special occasion dresses for high school proms, and casual dresses for family reunions. She is especially proud of a funny clown outfit she created for a niece. She also constructs covers for chairs and sofas. For her home, she has made curtains and other house and wall decorations. Frances is also known for her crocheted bedspreads, pillow shams, and table dollies.

Source Material

Oral history, daughter Gwen Nix.
Oral history, Willie Frances Warren and Gwen Nix

L. L Lowin, *The Women's Garment Workers' Union,* in *Look for the Union Label,*
 ed. G. Tyler (New York: Columbia University Press, 1994).
Garment Workers', (Pub. 1924); G. Tyler, *Look for the Union Label.*

THE HIGH PRICE OF STARDOM

STARDOM in the entertainment world comes with a sky-high price tag these days. Although stars are making more than ever, their expenses to stay at the top are higher than ever. Sample items: $75,000 yearly for clothes, $2,000 for a song. Expenses take a fourth of every pay check.

Dorothy Dandridge's curve-caressing gown cost her $1,000.

Zelda Wynn Valdes. 1905–2001
After 60 years designing for celebrities, Zelda Wynn
Valdes joined the founding team of the Dance
Theatre of Harlem to design costumes for dancers
and help the fledgling performance group soar.

Zelda Barbour Wynn Valdes

Zelda Wynn, a quiet, calm person, was an exceptional businesswoman, musician, and dressmaker. She started out doing alterations to evening gowns for the who's who of stars, then, the first Playboy costume, and finally, designed for the world-trotting Dance Theatre of Harlem.

Singer, Joyce Bryant's gowns were so tight, she needed help to walk. Zelda designed dresses to enhance the female shape, and to give a sense of drama to Joyce's performance.

Zelda Barbour Wynn Valdes was born in 1905, in Chambersburg, Pennsylvania. Her Catholic school music training stayed with her all of her life. She moved with her brothers to White Plains, N.Y., and joined them in an alteration-tailoring shop. She later opened a shop of her own and had so many New York City clients that she moved the shop to 158th and Broadway.

Zelda Wynn understood that clothing could create a special look that made an image for a singer. In 1953, an article in *Our World Magazine* stated, "... Greatest asset in Joyce Bryant, a noted 1950 singer, had been her gowns, designed by Zelda." The article continued, "Zelda's gowns changed torch singer, Joyce Bryant's career. When Zelda met Joyce, she was wearing bouffant, 'sweet' dresses and was singing 'sweet' songs," Zelda said. "Joyce liked it that way because she was religious and didn't want to change." However, Zelda convinced her that she had been hiding her biggest asset—her curvaceous figure. Out went the bouffant dresses and sweet song numbers. Zelda began making fabulous sexy gowns for Joyce. Sophisticated, provocative, sexy songs replaced the old music. Joyce's gowns were so low-cut, that audiences often breathlessly expected them to slip and really "show," but that did not happen. From then on, Joyce's career began to skyrocket.

Joyce was not the only one to rely on Zelda for show-stopping gowns. Actresses Ruby Dee, Carol Channing, Diahann Carroll, and singers Eartha Kitt, Damita Jo, Billie Holiday, and contralto Marian Anderson, and others were customers. In a 1995 interview with Edward Shoelwer, Director of the Dance Theatre of Harlem, Zelda said: "I made [actress] Constance Bennett's gown when she was to be presented to Queen Elizabeth."

COURTESY OF JIM BYERS

Other stars who enjoyed Ms. Wynn's work included singer Sarah Vaughan and dancer Josephine Primis, who could regularly be seen going into Zelda Wynn's shop on upper Broadway in Manhattan. Zelda's shop was the first black-owned business on Broadway. She later opened a store in a prime location downtown between 56th and 57th Streets. The shop was called "Chez Zelda." Zelda enjoyed talking about all the people who enjoyed her display windows. Many of them would helpfully suggest that she sell more gloves, accessories, etc., and informed her where to go in the garment district to purchase the items.

Zelda was a stickler for perfection. She did all the cutting and fitting for each garment. At night, after her seven employees had gone, she did the sewing. Zelda prided herself on not having lost a customer. Some felt she was expensive; others did not seem to mind. Nevertheless, whatever she charged, her customers knew that her designs were important to their careers, and they swore by her.

This shirred material is a trademark Zelda look.

Zelda fashioned the entire wardrobe of Edna May Robinson, wife of Sugar Ray Robinson, the famous 1950 boxer and national celebrity. Formerly a dancer, Edna May accompanied him to various clubs and openings. Mrs. Robinson wore Zelda's hostess gowns at home, and evening gowns and hand-knit suits on other occasions.

Dorothy Dandridge, Zelda's customer of long standing, was one of the first stars to recognize Zelda's artistry. Zelda Wynn Valdes, designer and dressmaker, visualized every woman as slim. Her skin-tight dresses were feminine yet sexy in every detail. Zelda also designed for Mrs. "Nat" King Cole, opera singer Jessye Norman, Josephine Baker, Gladys Knight, and for singer Ella Fitzgerald. "Edna Robinson recommended me to Ms. Fitzgerald when she was going to sing at the Apollo Theater in New York. I was able to measure her once, but thereafter she was so busy that she didn't have the time. She would order—always in a rush—and I would study photos of her and guess her increasing size. She always said they fit and she'd order more, always three at

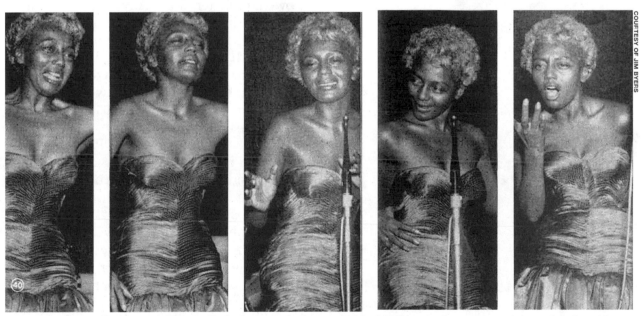

Joyce was one of the first singers to really look aggressively sexy. Zelda felt this was her strong point, and designed her dresses to emphasize that "look."

a time. I never had more than three to four days to finish the gowns. I am pleased to say that I never missed a delivery," Zelda said.

Zelda helped to found NAFAD, the National Association of Fashion and Accessory Designers, the organization of black designers and others in the fashion industry that was started through the auspices of Mary McLeod Bethune, president of Bethune-Cookman College in Florida. (See reference note.) Black designers were not allowed to join general business groups. Bethune felt that it was important to have a group to support and train African American designers. Zelda was president of the New York chapter in the 1950s. Many of the other designers featured in this book were or are members of NAFAD.

Wynn was also active in New York politics. She supported the Rev. Adam Clayton Powell, minister of the Abyssinian Baptist Church. She started doing fund-raising fashion shows for him and his church. She even toyed with the idea of joining him in Washington when he was elected a congressman, but, in her interview with Schoelwer, she said she had just married and "it was just too much."

Zelda worked on the first Playboy bunny costumes. Hugh Hefner later asked her to do the first fashion show at a Playboy Club, She told Ed Schoelwer, "Hefner started doing shows in all the Playboy Clubs."

In the 1980s, Zelda slowed down her business activities. She did designs, but she also trained people to sew for the Poverty Program. Arthur Mitchell heard of her and asked her to design and sew costumes for his new dance company. In 1995, Malik

Joyce Bryant mostly did night club work, Zelda would sometimes have to be there to help her get into the tight dresses.

Ducard quoted Wynn in a Newsday article: "I was 65 years old." She became the matriarch to Mitchell and the Dance Theatre of Harlem.

The Dance Theatre of Harlem (DTH) was founded in 1969 by ballet dancers Arthur Mitchell and Karen Shook. From an initial enrollment of just thirty students, the DTH has grown to a registration of over seven hundred students per year. The school, located on 152nd Street, in upper Manhattan, has emerged as a leading arts education center and as a dance training institute. The dancers perform classical, modern, and period dance pieces and tour the United States, Europe, and the world.

Zelda training sewing students in her work as a teacher in the Poverty Programs.

Zelda had not done costumes before, but she quickly converted her designing skills and trained her staff as well to make the costumes for the corps de ballet. Working sometimes night and day, sometimes sleeping in her basement offices, she literally lived and breathed DTH. She traveled to over twenty-two countries with the troupe and even sold in their gift shop after performances.

Zelda was a valued DTH staffer. She contributed her own money to the Dance Company, and she solicited funds from her celebrity clients. She convinced contralto singer Marian Anderson, for whom she had designed in the 1950s, to serve as a member of the Dance Theatre of Harlem Board. Ms. Anderson brought prestige and contacts from the arts community to the company.

Zelda worked every day for DTH until 2000 when, in her mid-nineties, she retired. After a long and varied career, she died in October 2001.

COURTESY OF JIM BYERS

Joyce Bryant credited Zelda with her popularity. 1952, cover of Our World *magazine.*

Reference Note

Mary McLeod Bethune (1875–1955): An African American educator and lecturer who was born poor and went to a local school in her hometown of Mayesville, South Carolina. She later received a scholarship to the Moody Bible Institute in Chicago. Mary Bethune taught at various schools, married Albert L. Bethune, and opened a small school in Daytona, Florida. This school later merged with another school to become the Bethune-Cookman School, with Bethune as president. She was active in politics and was an advisor on women and African American affairs to President and Mrs. Franklin Delano Roosevelt. One of her last achievements was to organize various African American women's clubs into the National Council of Negro Women and to encourage the founding of National Association of Fashion and Accessory Designers, [NAFAD].

Source Material

Our World, June, 1953; cover, and p. 43; Schomburg Library, NYC

Jim Byers, film maker-biographer; biography of Joyce Bryant, singer.

Librarian DTH, Robert Garland, Vernon Ross, production Director, Dance Theatre of Harlem; Jerome Grant, staff.

Collection: Jerome Robbins Dance Collection, NYC Public Library. Interview with Edward Schoelwer, Director of the DTH, 1990, for oral history project for the Jerome Robbins Dance Collection: NYC Public Library

Interviews:

Joy Elliott, writer, Reuters, Intl.

Lady Sara Lou Harris, leading model in 1950s.

Ersa Poston, political activist, 1950s, NYC.

Joyce Bailey, Black Fashion Museum, WDC.

Photographers: Moneta Sleet; Wil Blanche.

CHARLENE JOHNSTON

Rose is now in her late eighties and has wonderful stories to tell about designing for American celebrities.

Rose Batson

Rosenda Inez Segundo was born in New York City on May 27, 1912. She was one of four children born to Juan Segundo of Ponce, Puerto Rico, and Marie Bacote-Segundo of Charleston, South Carolina. Rose, or Rosie as her clients and friends know her, learned the skills and arts of sewing from her mother who had many customers in Charleston and in New York City.

Count Basie and his wife were socially active. She was expected to make fashion "statements" in specially designed outfits and coordinated hats

Rose expressed herself in the arts. At seven years old, she was an accomplished dancer. She won a small part in the movie "The Ne'er Do Wells," which starred the popular actress Lila Leads.

Later she was the first (known) black clerical employee hired by Macy's department store in New York City. Rose continued her second business as a designer-dressmaker by sewing for such celebrities as Lena Horne, Perry Como's wife, and Catherine Basie, Count Basie's wife. She also designed for the popular 1960s group, the Cowsills. In addition, she produced large fashion shows for community groups. Usually, the extravagant shows were held at the downtown Hilton Hotel. Fashion shows were then and now good sources of income for charity groups. The shows provided a wide audience for her designs.

Her designs were also featured in the Ebony Fashion Show, which was started in the 1950s and continues today in venues in large American cities, the Bahamas, and in Canada. The touring Ebony Fashion Show has become the largest fashion show in the U. S. The

Show has continued the tradition of many of African American designers who combined a passion for fashion with a commitment to social and political causes. The Ebony Show also helps local groups raise money for charity.

Rose's annual fashion extravaganza in New York drew crowds of fashion worshipers for years in the 1950s. She featured such models as Lois Bell, Herbie Moon, Bobby Marsan, Ann Porter-Cobb, and daughters and nieces: Judy Woodson, Vonnie Batson and Charlene Johnston.

Fashion shows in the 1950s and even now are major fundraisers for civic and professional groups. Here, Rose Batson is with a committee planning a large fashion show

Batson designed costumes for performer Irving Burgie who composed the songs "Jamaica Farewell," "Day-O," etc., which readers may remember as songs that made Harry Belafonte famous.

Rose also had a career in oil painting. She exhibited her works in various venues in New York and, when she retired, in Florida.

Rose married Louis Batson in l933. Their union produced two daughters, Yvonne, who works in the movie and TV animation industry, and

A Rosa Batson design. Charlene Johnston wore this checkered wool creation in 1970s

An Indian sari-inspired dress designed by Rosa Batson and worn by daughter Charlene Johnston

An emerald green evening gown and matching coat created by Rosa Batson and worn by Judy Woodson in the l970s

Charlene, a retired dental health professor, who did professional folk dancing and designing in her youth.

Now 90 years old, and wheel chair bound due to strokes, Rose still has the most beautiful smile and can spin stories of the wonderful life she has led and the exciting people she has met. She lives in Burbank, California with her Vonnie. She is a great looking candidate should there be Hollywood auditions for fashionable senior citizens.

Source Material

Interview with Charlene Johnston and Leanna Freeman

LIBRARY OF CONGRESS

Perry Como, popular singer of the 1950s and 1960s.

Rose Batson designed this lovely wedding dress for her granddaughter, Leanna Freeman.

The red door opens to the world of Toast and Strawberries and the talented designers who make it unique.

Part III: Their Legacy

Toast and Strawberries Boutique

When I was asked to produce a black history fashion show, it was as though I had come full circle. I graduated from Temple University in Philadelphia as a history major, and I was aware of black women who had been designers for famous black and white women. I seized the opportunity to learn more about them and to share their stories with a black and white audience.

My interest in fashion designers may have come from my mother, Eloise Scott Reed of Virginia and Philadelphia, who graduated from the University of Pennsylvania in the early 1950s and wanted to be either a fashion or interior designer. After marriage and two children and with racism limiting her employment options, she taught art in the Philadelphia school system.

Rosemary E. Reed Miller in newly opened shop at R Street, N.W., in 1966

She, like her mother, her grandmother and great-grandmother, created fabulous clothes. I never understood when people would say, negatively, "You look just like your mother, etc." I took it as a compliment to look as good as my mother looked and dressed.

Initially, I worked as a journalist and traveled, but my opening the shop Toast and Strawberries was probably "in my genes." In 1966, after working in Jamaica,

West Indies as a journalist and accessory designer, I established Toast and Strawberries, a unique gift and fashion boutique at 2009 R Street, N.W. Washington, D.C. I had been selling my own designs and representing other designers at various trade shows. Had just married, and I was somewhat tired of traveling to different cities. I thought I could open a showroom/shop. Buyers could come and see the clothing and gift designs, and I would pay the rent by selling to retail customers.

I was then representing various artists, and many more came to me. I felt it was important to showcase them so that we would not lose them and their talent to New York, California, or to Europe. At Toast and Strawberries, we looked for a "now" idea, but we wanted our dresses to last for years—years of good design and years of good wear. I am proud to say that we have kept that promise. Customers frequently tell us that they have dresses in their closets from our shop that are five to twenty years old!

Reed-Miller and Pamela Carriere, Toast and Strawberries manager, in the shop at R Street, NW, in 1966

We tried to bring to our shop—and therefore to Washington—young designers (I am not sure why the designers had to be "young," but most of us were in our twenties) from various regions of the U.S., Hong Kong, and Australia. I found a press release that listed our designers as: "Celle from Pottstown, Pennsylvania; Crispin recently from London, now of California; Rita Johnson, from Arlington, Virginia, but recently of Paris; Andrea Mahaffy, of Maryland's School of Design; Paula Stafford of Australia's Gold Coast; Knobkerry's Sarah Penn of New York City; and Betty Pair of Washington."

That same 1966 release reported that our models were: "Deane Gross, Sharon Thomas, Sandy Barrett, Helen Moody, and sisters Mina and Mei Ling Smith from the Philippines." I was also pleased to see that the production and arts credits of the release noted that Anna Rice and Jean Houlihan, now deceased, and photographer Franklin Mink were working with us.

We—Jean Houlihan, Pamela Carriere, Elaine Heffernan, and I—thought it was important to combine our interest in fashions with our 1960s ideal-

Models Carolyn and Deane in one of our evening outdoor fashion shows. Because most of the staff had been active in the Civil Rights Movement, we had our models carry signs—only this time they said: "Dresses or Guys Welcome."

ism. We felt it was important to show that talent had no limits—male, female, white, and black. We advertised in black and white newspapers, used black and white models in our ads, and found and sold a baby-back carrier. "As a woman and as a mother," I wrote, "I know how much our society tends to block fathers from their children's care, thereby relegating women to servitude and denying men important experiences with the nurturing process." Heavy duty for 1968, but fairly relevant even today!

We have also met many interesting customers over the years. I was intrigued, for example, to find a 1977 letter from socialite Barbara Gordon who put on a fashion show at the Woman's National Democratic Club, on New Hampshire Ave., N.W., in Washington, D.C., and that our assigned models had included Tipper Gore, wife of then Senator Albert Gore. We did not know of her then. We knew, or knew of the other guest models: Alma (wife of Rep. Charlie Rangel), Sweden's Countess Wachtmeister, Mrs. "Vicky" Smith Bagley, and Lady Ramsbotham, wife of the Ambassador of Great Britain. All became pleasant and enthusiastic customers.

I found that people were impressed when we said that we had various celebrities as customers. Angela Bofill, the singer, was quiet and pleasant when she came into the shop. In the early 1990s, Bill Washington of Dimensions, Inc., called and asked me if I was starstruck. I do not think I am, but I also knew of 'stars' not paying for clothes, so I asked him who the "star" was. He said, "Anita Baker." I had not heard of her and asked him who she was. I learned that she and Luther Vandross were starting a tour in Washington. She needed alterations and a cape. I soon found that everybody knew of her, but it meant that we dealt with her as a human being.

We have also sold to Roberta Flack, through Ruth Jackson's introduction; and Aretha Franklin, via Cynthia Warfield. We enjoyed doing special designs for Mrs. Caspar Weinberger, wife of the former secretary of defense; Mrs. Roger Mudd, wife of the newscaster; Mrs. Art Buchwald; Renée

Countess Wachtmeister and Lady Frances Ramsbotham were wives of the ambassadors of Sweden and Great Britain, respectively.

The shop was located on the corner of Connecticut and 'R' Streets, N.W. A tea shop is now in the location.

Poussaint, television newscaster and film maker; and legions of others. What we discovered was that various people saw such a wide variety of people in the store that they stopped in to "feel in touch with D.C.."

We also put on workshops, hosted book signings for authors and poets (the deceased Trinidadian poet Wilfred Carty comes to mind), produced miniature concerts in the store, put on fashion shows in different cities, and spoke to the wide world through panels and media interviews. However, researching and writing *Threads of Time* provides another opportunity to do our business—sell clothes and work with small designers—because they are our reason for being. We buy from regular firms in California (Carole Dolighan, Whispers, hand-painted lovelies), New York, and Rhode Island, and the firm, Adini, originally named "India Imports," from which we have

Designer, Roxie Munro illustrates an African caftan.

A classic dress designed by Roxie Munro for Toast in the 1970s.

Roxie Munro later illustrated books and cover designs for New Yorker magazine.

Judge Harry T. Alexander joins two models wearing Indian-imported summer outfits, in front of the old 'R' Street Toast location.

bought for over thirty years. Their materials had the floral border prints—the 1970's "flower child" look.

Managing the day-to-day business is necessary, but as a daughter of teachers who thought community work was "normal," I know that writing *Threads of Time*, is necessary to ensure that we are "doing the job."

The late David Clark, formerly chair, Washington, D.C., City Council, and Rosemary E. Reed Miller wearing a Joyce Scott necklace in the 1980s.

The current location of Toast and Strawberries at 1608 Conn. Ave., N.W., Dupont Circle.

Viola Leak, art educator, lecturer, and performance artist.

Part IV:
Designers Who Have Touched Toast and Strawberries

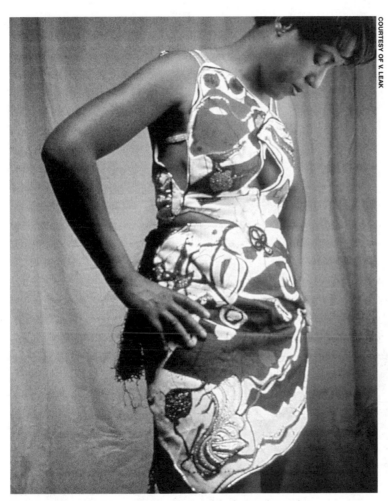

Dress shown combines fiber, cotton, with decorative paint and applique.

Viola Burley Leak

Viola Burley Leak received her B.A. in Art from Fisk University in Tennessee, a B.F.A. in Fashion Design from Pratt Institute in New York City, an M.A. in Creative Arts and Studio Printmaking from Hunter College of the City University of New York, and a M.F.A. in Printmaking from Howard University, Washington, D.C..

Viola has studied with some of America's most celebrated black artists: Aaron Douglas, Robert Blackburn, Charles White, and Romare Bearden.

She has worked as a toy designer for Ideal Toy Company and as an advertising artist for BBD&O Advertising Agency. As an educator, she has taught at North Carolina Central University and is presently teaching art in the Washington, D.C. public schools, and she is an assistant professor in Fashion Design for Howard University and for the University of the District of Columbia.

Burley Leak's work is provocative and exciting. Whether she is designing a large quilt installation or a wearable art coat, she utilizes bright colors and a myriad of textiles and textures. Viola once said, "I like to surprise my customers. Whether I am designing a shawl or a quilt, I like to give them an item that they will enjoy. I hope they will see in it something different each time they wear it."

Although she sells her clothing designs to stores, she also does commissions for collections or for industrial sites. Her work can be seen in the World Federation Building, in the Manufacturer's Trust Company, and in the Atlanta Life Insurance Company.

Appliqued wool Jacket by Viola Burley Leak. Stitches add dimension.

Wearable art design by Viola B. Leak. Zuni Indian doll applique.

COURTESY OF V. LEAK

Recently, the artist has come full circle in combining textile and print making techniques to explore black heritage through tapestries, soft sculpture, quilts, and dolls. This newer work presents such subjects as a field hand picking cotton, the Alabama church bombings, and other significant historical events. Her work consists, in both form and content, on the possibility of art that possesses beauty and long-lasting social significance.

Viola Burley Leak's work has been exhibited in the Smithsonian Renwick Gallery American Crafts Museum; the American Museum of Contemporary Crafts, New York City; the Bronx Museum, NY; DuSable Museum, Chicago, Illinois; University of Erlanger, Germany; the National Theatre, Lagos, Nigeria; and numerous other venues. Her work has also been featured in

The wool and leather appliqued coat by Viola combine to make a beautiful wearable art piece.

many publications, video series, and in art journals.

As Burley Leak once described her own guiding philosophy: "I approach each work—a full scarf, quilt, or a large print—as an experience which begins with a concept that is allowed to evolve into its own entity and statement." Perhaps it is precisely this commitment to ongoing change, guided by the wisdom of the past and the present that is responsible for the enduring success of this artist and designer.

Coat designed by Viola Burley Leak. Applique is "Senufo" symbol, inspired by West African fertility doll.

Viola has exhibited at the art and crafts museum of the Smithsonian—the Renwick Gallery, which is located across from the White House in a classic 1890 restored mansion.

Source Material

Personal interviews with the artist.

Cindy Williams designs both clothing and gift accessories for people searching for unusual items.

Cindy Williams

Cindy Williams was born in Washington, D.C., and attended Margaret Mary Washington School for Design Training. She continued her education in fashion merchandising at the University of the District of Columbia and later apprenticed at the fashion firm of Vera-Christian.

Card designed by Cindy Williams. "Cards opened a whole other design world to me," she said.

"My family are all creative people, who fix, build, play, sing, and enjoy the art of life," Cindy said. She grew up making doll clothes and seeing her mother make clothes from fabrics at hand. "I guess I grew up thinking that everyone made coats from draperies and bedspreads." "I've had tons of work experience—from being a flight attendant to a school bus driver—when my son was young. After traveling full circle and being in a bad car accident, I'm back to first loves of designing clothes, creating interesting hair styles, creating accessories and greeting cards—even doing large paintings."

Cindy is widely known for having an eye for elaborate and unusual fabrics. She designs hats, pillows, large dolls, and suits influenced by the textiles of Asia and Africa. She now works out of a studio, but for many years, she had a store in Northwest Washington, called "Just One." "I lost my lease, and I wasn't sure what to do, but I now find designing for people and wholesaling to various stores quite satisfying," Cindy said.

Ms. Williams has participated in many fashion shows. She has been featured in various fashion publications and has been a guest on local television shows. "I would like to get back to doing a yearly show. It is hard work, but you are able to get your friends and customers together, and see how your new line really works, " Cindy said. "Recently, I've been commissioned to design covers for journals, decorative boxes, and bags," Cindy said. "Next, I have in mind to write a few books, and to write and produce a stage play."

The internationally famous singer Chaka Khan has bought some of Cindy's dolls. "I call my dolls 'Real Kids' because I'm inspired by children I see on the streets." Marita Golden, the writer, is also a favorite doll customer.

Her one-of-a-kind greeting cards have become collector's items. Comedian, television host, and writer Bertice Berry has bought her cards. She also has sold them to Betty Currie, secretary to former President

Cindy Williams also paints. This is a 4ft. X 4 ft. painting that she exhibited in 1999.

Clinton, who buys the birthday cards for friends and colleagues. One of Ms. Currie's friends, who especially enjoyed Cindy's cards, was movie actress Whoopi Goldberg.

Cindy's inspirational projects leave no doubt that this unique and multi-talented artist and designer will continue to produce work that, in any medium, will stand at the forefront of contemporary fashion and culture.

Source Material

Personal correspondence with the designer.

The doll is almost life-size. Cindy Williams calls her dolls "Real Kids." Real children inspire her to create her vision of them.

"I always enjoy finding guys who like my designs. So many guys tell me that they can't find interesting clothes," said Cindy.

*Pamela is known for her detailed special occasion
outfits and wedding dresses*

Pamela Botchway

Pamela Botchway is a certified schoolteacher, who was born in Ghana and now lives and designs in the Washington, D.C., area. She holds a B.S. in textile and clothing from the University of the District of Columbia. Pamela has shared her love of clothing and design with students at the Washington Academy of Fashion and at the Phyllis Wheatley YWCA.

Botchway's artistic designs have won critical praise throughout the metropolitan area. Her work is showcased in various Washington boutiques: Timbuktu and Kobos' Designs in the international Adams-Morgan area; and at Toast and Strawberries in Dupont Circle.

These two African print pieces were designed by Pamela Botchway. Pamela usually creates a hat to coordinate with her designs.

Pamela's pieces have been featured in *Washington Living* magazine and in many fashion shows. She has participated in smaller shows, such as Capital Artist Productions and the United Women of Ghana, but she is proud to participate annually in the larger Congressional Black Caucus fashion show and the National Association of Fashion and Accessory shows. The Congressional Black Caucus (CBC) fashion show, a fundraiser given annually with audiences of five thousand, is one of the largest fashion shows in America.

"I had heard about NAFAD," Pamela said, "and after graduating, I immediately applied for membership." NAFAD was organized in 1950 under the sponsorship of the National Council of Negro Women as a professional organization for the growing number of black women in the fashion industry. There are over twenty city chapters serving members throughout the U. S. with yearly show attendance ranging from three to five hundred people.

From concept to the last hem stitch, Pamela's designs straddle several cultures—African, European, and American. "I especially enjoy the opportunity to design wedding dresses. You can really show your creative talent on the canvas of a bridal dress and veil," Pamela said.

Her clients have included famed singing group Sweet Honey in the Rock, Mrs. Caspar Weinberger, wife of the former secretary of defense in the Reagan administration, noted Professor Eleanor Traylor, head of the Howard University Department of English, Baroness Stakelberg, and Nobel Prize author Toni Morrison, among others.

Ms. Botchway is often asked by various groups and the Smithsonian Museum of African Art to demonstrate skirt and head wrapping. Ms. Botchway observed, "Wrap skirts, which are ideal for Africa's warm climates,

Pamela's daughter is helping to finish a wedding dress.

A wedding dress done by Botchway for Toast and Strawberries.

are popular in America. I've always been intrigued by the way fashion crosses over to many groups in many countries." She notes that caftans and wrap skirts are worn by women for casual wear, or in rich fabrics for fabulous evening affairs. "Head wraps also seem to be coming back", she said. "I see them on suburban girls as well as city women. I'm especially pleased to see some of the new singers wearing them. Hopefully, that means all sorts of women will be inspired to wear head wrappings with flare."

Source Material
Personal interview with the designer.

Botchway is known for her satin-trimmed wedding veils.

Bride and groom African-influenced outfits.

Saharah combines International fabrics and images into designs which can be worn by everyone everywhere.

Saharah

A two-piece Asian choli- inspired embroidered outfit suitable for a queen's court.

Saharah's Collection is a high fashion line of clothing for men and women who are interested in expressing themselves artistically. She also appeals to the many people who embrace their ethnic and religious heritage as they progress through life spiritually, intellectually, and economically.

Her feeling is that the desire for a mode of dress that is more in tune with one's self-expression increases as one's knowledge increases. Saharah designs use European, Asian, and African influences. Traveling extensively and researching traditional garb, Saharah creates designs that combine lifestyle and cultural heritage.

Saharah has been especially interested in full-size figures, the forgotten women. Many of her best customers wear larger sizes, and she works artfully to enhance and flatter their figures. She concentrates on the drape and fall of fabric, applies hand painting, and uses interesting textures to create a lovely canvas that conceals what some people might consider body flaws. In Saharah's work, the so-called body flaw becomes an occasion for the designer to enhance the natural fashion possibilities of the full body and bring out the inherent beauty of all body sizes and shapes.

Her collection represents an important transition from a strictly female sexual focus to one which draws the admirer into the realm of pure beauty. Saharah concentrates on the texture and feel of the fabric, applying hand painting and handprinting to use the clothing as a canvas. A flattering advantage occurs naturally in Saharah's artful styles. The body's 'flaws' are concealed; its overall appearance is enhanced.

Born in Washington, D.C., Saharah attended the Rhode Island School of Design and Howard University for design degrees. She has found that travel is important to her design inspirations. On trips to Asia, the Middle East, and Africa, she learned how to block print, which has become her trademark, and how to shape her clothing and use different color palettes.

A strapless design with a dramatic shawl by Saharah.

She includes the traditional Shalwar Kineez—tunic and pants—in her regular collection. Saharah also has a dress with the look and feel of a sari, but she adds her own unique touch—the woman's middle is covered. And again, long before the scarf or "pashmina" craze, Saharah featured special woven shawls with her ensembles as part of the "look."

Saharah's clothing has been featured in Nordstrom and other department stores, but she prefers smaller boutiques that are better suited for limited edition garments. She has a private studio in her suburban Washington D.C., home. Elements of her lines are often made in Pakistan where fabrics and prints are unique.

Saharah is founder of the nonprofit arts organization, The Global Family, which is dedicated to encouraging mothers and daughters to work together in puppet making, dance, theatre, and performance. Her work with her filmmaker husband and creative daughter has inspired her to produce children's and menswear for special occasions.

*Pantaloons are fun
and traditional
around the world.*

Saharah's combination of fabrics and prints are her focal point.

Her costuming and design skills have brought her to the attention of Aretha Franklin, Danny Glover, singer T'Keya Crystal Khema, and Washington, D.C.'s own singing group, Sweet Honey in the Rock. Professional groups, such as the LaVerne Dancers, All About Creativity, and the Children's Arts Ensemble, have also used her design talents.

Source Material

Personal interviews with the designer.

COURTESY OF SAHARAH DESIGNS

Saharah at a trunk show in a department store. She has on a traditional outfit. The model is wearing a loose, mid-length mud cloth vest from West Africa.

Joyce Scott. Mardi Gras shirt. Fibers, beads and sequins. 1977 Private collection.

Joyce Scott

Fiber artist and sculptor Joyce Scott was born in 1948, in Baltimore, Maryland, to Charlie and Elizabeth Talford Scott. Her mother is an artist and quilter. Elizabeth Talford Scott and her daughter Joyce have had group exhibits at the Smithsonian Renwick Gallery that houses the American crafts collection.

When mother and daughter decided to team up, the results are spectacular. They have had joint exhibits at the Fonda Del Sol Gallery in Washington, D.C., and, reaching an even wider audience, Elizabeth and

Author, Rosemary E. Reed Miller, wearing one of Joyce Scott's collage necklaces, 1978.

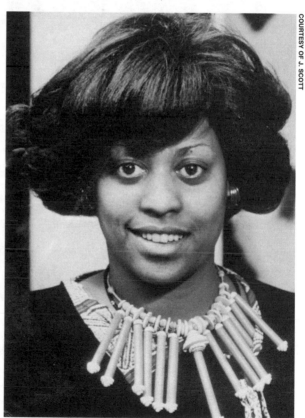

Washington print dealer Helen Jackson wearing a necklace by Joyce Scott in 1976.

Joyce Scott have had their life and work featured in a Maryland Public TV documentary.

Joyce went to public schools in Baltimore and undertook art studies at the Maryland Institute College of Art. She has a Master of Arts from the Instituto Allende in Mexico, and she has taught in various places around the world.

Joyce Scott has held residences in Art in many schools, including the Rhode Island School of Design, the Moore School of Art in Philadelphia,

"Plantation Quilt" executed and designed by Elizabeth and Joyce Scott. From an exhibit at Washington Gallery, Fonda del Sol, 1977.

"50-Year Quilt"—a five-foot square history of the Scott family. Designed by Elizabeth and Joyce Scott.

"Fortuna"   Joyce Scott looks at traditional Africa and playing card luck in this bead, glass, plastic and stone piece. Joyce is Baltimore's "Wonder Woman of Art." She is a singer, writer, sculptor, and storyteller, teacher, and an actress. 32" tall; 1999. Artist's private collection. Picture courtesy of Artist.

"Clara + Present. Joyce usually combines whimsy with a serious vision in her sculptures. 30" tall; Combination of bead, wire, glass, plastic and found pieces. 1999. Sculptor's private collection. Picture courtesy of Artist.

and the University of Hawaii. Her continuing studies include work at the Haystack Mountain School of Crafts in Deer Island, Maine.

Joyce's world of work includes sculpture, lithographs, large installations, and fiber arts. Her list of solo exhibits includes the Baltimore Museum of Art, the Corcoran Gallery of Art in Washington, D.C., the San Francisco Art Institute, the Brooklyn College of Art, the Franklin and Marshall College in Pennsylvania, and the Rapp Gallery in Scottsdale, Arizona.

In the foreword to the catalogue for her show at the Baltimore Museum of Art, in February 2000, Dr. Leslie King-Hammond wrote, ". . . Joyce traveled to Mali, Senegal, Gambia, and Morocco in 1978 . . . [her] curiosity about how artists in other cultures approach, interpret, and technically execute their own aesthetic modalities is central to her need to experience the world in order to better understand the nature of her own intentions. Her ventures have taken her to villages, towns, communities, and artist enclaves in Thailand, Hong Kong, Canada, Holland, England, Scotland, Hawaii, Jamaica, St. Martin, and Cuba."

Joyce also designs and creates "wearable art" clothing and jewelry. She writes and sings her own music and has written her own solo and group comic and satiric plays. Scott works hard and has fun in life. As she eloquently puts it, "This is my only chance . . . as a human being and I [am] supposed to run and chase it down. . . . This is Paradise—the fact that I don't have to separate my life from my work."

Source Material:

Baltimore Museum of Art Catalogue for February Show, 2000. King-Hammond, "Kickin' It with the Old Masters."

Patricia Jackson, founder of the firm, "Fashionably Yours," is one of Washington's knitwear designers.

Patricia Jackson

In each town, a clientele cherishes various designers. Pat Jackson is one of those special designers. She has been especially creative in the area of knits. Patricia says, "My knits are premium wools just like or better than the famous brands. In addition, when I do a creation for a customer, it is one of a kind."

Since 1980, she has been designing out of her large studio in Silver Spring, Maryland. She took Master Design classes in tailoring and knitting. "I start from scratch, and design the finished garment," she states. Jackson also crochets and knits sweaters, dresses, skirts, coats, and jackets.

Jeannette Knight, Pat's daughter, is modeling a Chanel-inspired outfit.

Jeanette Knight—wearing a textured silk-blend ensemble.

Customer service is a key focus of any business, and Pat's business, which is called "Fashionably Yours," is strong on service. "I have to keep things in balance because people can take advantage of a small business with their tales of woe, but I can do special designs in a short time period if one of my customers has a last minute occasion that is really important to her," Jackson has said.

Pat is a member of many design-related organizations: Knitting Guild of America; Who's Who Worldwide; National Association of Female Executives; International Fabricare Institute; National Association of Fashion Accessories and Designers (NAFAD); and D.C. Knitter Club, which she founded in 1984.

The mannequin is displaying one of Patricia Jackson's intricate, hand-finished silk knits.

She has received two awards from NAFAD for her design work. She exhibits her designs in their annual fashion show. Pat, over the years, has produced fashion shows for the American Cancer Society, and for various sororities such as the Alpha Kappa Alphas, and for the Deltas Sigma Thetas.

Pat designs for a wide range of women in the Washington, D.C., metropolitan area. She sells to many TV and other celebrities. One of her favorite customers is J. C. Hayward, a long established anchorperson on CBS television network. She has been commissioned to design for "Austin Mace," children's clothesline and Therese André, a French designer.

Pat feels that her talents come from a long line of knitters and sewers. Her grandaunt and her grandmother did beautiful crochet work. Pat relates the story about her great-aunt and grandmother who was white. "In the segregated days of Washington, D.C., in the l930s–40s, she would buy special fabrics and yarns from stores. She was able to go and pick out special pieces that the salespeople wouldn't let us 'colored' people dig for. She even sold to and did samples for G Street

Judy Knight, daughter of Patricia Jackson, in wool-blend evening outfit.

Fabrics, the leading notions and fabric store in the city. Her items were in the display windows. She and her sister-in-laws did the work. The store would display them as samples for their customers to order. Little did the store know that that white lady was married to a 'colored' man and her 'colored' relatives created the lovely works in their windows."

For years, Pat has had a large roster of knitting and sewing classes, which she holds in the large, well-appointed basement in her home. Margaret Jackson said,… "As a student, I found her to be a capable instructor, patient and understanding." The machines are expensive and somewhat complicated. Pat tries to get her students over the usual intimidation so they can concentrate on their designs.

Pat continues that family tradition by creating wonderful designs in fabric and in special yarns. "I even do special house decorative items, and I enjoy teaching my regular crochet and knitting classes, but I think the bridal is the most rewarding. You have an opportunity to really use your design and creative skills, and the dresses are part of a wonderful, special day in that person's life. It can't get much better that that."

*Rita Johnson Falkener has moved
from clothing design to commercial
interior design.*

Rita Johnson Falkener

Rita Johnson, right, wearing an African-inspired cotton print, shares a design idea with a model.

Born in Arlington, Virginia, Rita Falkener graduated from Pratt Institute of Design, New York City, and then studied design and fashion in Paris. She started her clothing business in Washington, D.C., where she created special designs and produced her own work for Toast and Strawberries and other stores in the Washington–Baltimore area. In the late 1970s, she moved to New York City and continued designing clothes. She sold to the boutique sections of various department stores and then created gift items and interiors for various commercial concerns.

"I realized that home furnishings engaged more of my design skills than clothing. I could find fabrics, textures, and interesting light and color concepts in the realm of a whole house, office, or building," Rita said. Rita started designing small accessories for wholesale home furnishing design houses. She went on to design whole rooms to showcase her talents in such prestigious venues as Kip's Bay Decorators Show House in New York City; the Woolworth Mansion; Rynwood; Castles on the Sound, Long Island; and the Bloomingdale Mansion in Westchester.

Rita Johnson used an Indonesian-African cotton border print for this 1970s summer dress

Models Helen Moody
and Sharon Thomas
have fun in two of
Rita Johnson's designs.

She also participated in the design of "Space for Photography" at the Light Gallery on Fifth Avenue in Manhattan and other major promotional displays for the window treatment firms of Levolor Lorentzen, Hunter Douglas, and the Sperry Hutchinson Corporation.

"I went on to be certified to do institutional work. Offices, large buildings, and hospitals take a different slant on interior design. Your materials have to be more functional, solid, welcoming, muted but pleasantly colored, and designed for long-term wear and tear." Now Rita's work with her firm, Falkener-Stuetley, is almost wholly hospitals, office and other commercial work.

COURTESY OF GWEN NIX

COURTESY OF GWEN NIX

Rita is still excited about her work. "Each job is challenging—time constraints, budgets, design and use, your vendors, your contractors, and your client. . . .You must be quite 'organized' to make everything and everyone come together in a timely way to execute the whole project. It still is the most exciting world I can think of for an artist." She and her partner, Stan Stuetley, have been featured in various publications: the *New York Times,* the *New York Post,* the *Washington Star, Black Enterprise, Cosmopolitan, House Beautiful, House and Garden, Interior Design,* and *New York Magazine.* In the *House Beautiful Collector's Edition* that celebrated 100 years of style (November 1966), they were listed among the 101 most influential designers in America.

Ms. Falkener lives in a lovely, four-story brownstone office-studio in Brooklyn Heights. She is married to Waldo Falkener, an attorney.

Sources:

Interview with Mrs. Johnson Falkener, 2001

Rosemary Reed babypacking infant daughter, Sabrina, wearing a Rita Johnson two-piece ribbon-trimmed and wool jersey outfit. We were the first to sell this baby carrier. It brought us national attention.

SARA PENN

Sara Penn continues to create wearable art accessories from exotic and antique cloths and jewelry.

Sara Penn

Sara Penn was born in Pittsburgh. Her first start in the fashion world was as a social worker. She graduated from Spelman College in Atlanta, Georgia, studied advanced social casework at the University of Pittsburgh, and earned her Masters in Social Work from Atlanta University.

"After working in New York City in the 1960s, I was drawn to ethnic textiles and clothing. I met various importers and decided I would open a gallery and ethnographic enterprise specializing in international art, textiles, and furniture."

Writer Joy Elliott quotes Ms. Penn, in a November 1969 article in the *Washington Post,* "I was disappointed with the scope of the poverty program, so after 15 years as a social worker, I decided to make clothes for my own boutique."

Ms. Penn joined forces with two partners when she first opened the store Knobkerry: African American, Olive Wong, who had a degree from Vassar in theatrical clothing designs, and Fume Schmidt, an Asian

Models wear Sara's outfits at show for Smithsonian in Washington, D.C.. 1970s .

Sara standing in her trademark imports from the Middle East, Asia and Africa.

American, whose degree was from the University of Hawaii in Dance and English.

"It was a small shop. I could be at the shop evenings and weekends—when you're young you have all sorts of energy," Ms. Penn said. She and her colleagues were lucky. The shop was a success. Various newspapers wrote about the shop, and she exhibited her clothes in fashion shows at the jazz club, the Village Vanguard, and in Washington, D.C., at the Smithsonian.

The name "Knobkerry" is from George Bernard Shaw's *Adventures of a Black Girl in Search of God*. A "knobkerry" is an intricately decorated beaded Zulu hunting stick used in South and East Africa. The quest of western, new world blacks for an identity inspired Ms. Penn to choose the name "Knobkerry" for the new shop. For fashion designers Sarah, Olive, and Fume, the knobkerry was a symbolic link to various identities and cultures.

"I also took courses at the Fashion Institute of Technology (FIT) in New York City, and classes at the Alliance Française. The courses at FIT helped me with my sewing and designs, and the language course helped me in traveling and dealing with importers and vendors," Ms. Penn related.

Sara Penn standing in front of her lower Eastside fashion establishment in 1980s

The famous model Lauren Hutton wearing one of Sara's designs from India on the cover of the Saturday Evening Post magazine, 1970s.

Over the years, she has moved the shop and joined other partners, but the basic idea of selling textiles and art from Africa, Asia, and the Americas has continued. Knobkerry started out in the East Village, on St. Marks Place. Later, as the rents increased in that area, she moved to Soho, further south in lower Manhattan.

"Ms. Penn has been a Marco Polo traversing hemispheres to dig up exotica. In one corner there are (Indian) saris, (Japanese) kimonos, in another, 19th century Japanese cabinets." states Dulcie Leimach, in a 1994 *New York Times* article. "Elsewhere around the shop are textiles

Beverly Johnson was one of the first brown-skinned African American models to get national exposure. She is wearing one of Ms. Penn's import designs.

Beverly Johnson in a cotton eyelet embroidery outfit imported by Sara from Nigeria.

from places like Sierra Leone, Mali, China, Indonesia, Colombia, and Mexico. On the walls are colorful 'fighting flags' from the Fanti people of Ghana, priced between $2,500 and $3,000", Mrs. Leimach added.

Knobkerry literally has a place in the history of African American and ethnic culture shops. Before 1965, there might have been an "ethnic" shop in either an East or West Coast city, but Knobkerry was one of the first with a wide range of designs, textiles, and imports. The display of these various items was always creative, and they were sold to a wide clientele. Knobkerry was also highlighted in fashion and cultural coverage by various journals. Such publicity gave Sarah Penn credibility among African Americans with a growing interest in expressing their own cultural identity through clothing and furniture accessories.

In a *Washington Post* article, Joy Elliott quotes Ms. Penn as saying, "I do all the buying for the shop, and I will pass up a bargain or a best-seller in a minute to retain the originality of our display and in our collection. I think black designers, like black musicians, should dig into their origins for [their] inspirations. It would help to 'signpost' our current quest for identity and bring something different to Western fashion."

SARA PENN

Seminole inspired — S. Penn

Sara exhibited her wearable art designs in galleries in New York City.

Sara Penn has sponsored textile exhibits and gallery shows. In the mid-1990s, she sponsored a successful showing by the internationally renowned black artist David Hammons who has exhibited in galleries and museums in Austria, the Netherlands, and the U. S., among others. She has also created special showings of kilm rugs from Afghanistan, Iran, and Turkey and exhibits of rugs from Bukhara, Uzbekistan, in West Central Asia.

Over the years, a shopper at Knobkerry might have run into Louise Nevelson, the sculptor, Willie Smith, black clothing firm designer, guitarist Jimi Hendrix, jazzmen Ornette Coleman or Pharaoh Saunders. Knobkerry was an "in" store for New York City's cultural elite.

Volunteers used to work at the store to learn about fashion, but they also hoped to meet celebrities such as Mia Farrow, or Mrs. Jules Stein, wife of the

Broadway composer. The volunteers joined a pool of part-time sales clerks that included teenagers Sara advised as a social worker in the city's anti-poverty programs.

"I realize" Sara has said, "that I reflect my great-grand aunt, Sadie Lee in Pleasant Valley, Alabama, who followed Booker T. Washington's idea of skilled training for newly freed slaves. (See reference note.) She taught quilting and sewing. She opened a training school there that grew to have over two hundred students."

Sara has just re-opened Knobkerry on East 6th Street. She had many of her carvings and textiles in storage. She will continue selling to various import stores in Manhatten. Toast and Strawberries contiues to carry her intricate, antique fabric handbag designs.

Whatever Sara does in the future, we know it will have a special sense of design and creativity. Opening her store in New York City in 1965, a mecca for visitors from all over the world, gave her customers an opportunity for unique expression, and her success was an inspiration to other merchants who wanted to open ethnic-focused stores throughout the world.

The interiors of Sara's shops were as interesting as the clothes.

This jacket was on the cover of the brochure for a wearable art show in Bryn Mawr, Pennsylvania.

VVBFM

Lois Alexander Lane, founder of the Black Fashion Museum.

Part V: The Black Fashion Museum

In 1979, Lois Alexander, a Washington, D.C. native, opened the Black Fashion Museum on 126th Street in Harlem, New York City, as an educational affiliate of the Harlem Institute of Fashion training college.

Ms. Alexander, who was a noted designer in the 1950s–60s, wanted to have a national repository for the work of black fashion designers. She felt it was important to highlight and promote the talents of historical and contemporary dressmakers and designers.

While doing research on her master's thesis, *"The Role of the Negro in Retailing in New York City from 1863 to the Present,"* Mrs. Alexander found little information on the contributions of black designers. As a result of her research, she felt it necessary to dispel the myth that blacks are new to fashion, and she wanted to share with the black community another facet of its heritage.

"No one thought there was enough material to have a museum," she remembered. When she became ill, her daughter Joyce Alexander Bailey moved the museum to Washington, DC, in the early 1990s. It is now located near the U Street, NW corridor, which is historically known as "Black Broadway."

In her 1982 book, *Blacks in the History of Fashion,* Lois K. Alexander relates how she went from city to city, across the United States presenting the idea of collecting either current designers' clothes, or clothes from the 1800–1900s. She was able to collect enough to fill the museum on 157 West 126th Street. She was able to interest models, society women, mainstream department store staff, fashion types, such as Susan Taylor, editor of Essence Magazine, and Audrey Smaltz, who, in those times did the commentary for the Ebony Fashion Show to join her and her effort to open the Museum.

The Black Fashion Museum (BFM) is the only one of its kind. Its current location in the Shaw area of Washington, D.C. was, according to the National Park Service, a station on the Underground Railroad. In the early

1900s, the location was a meeting place for the Ladies' Relief Association and was later the Sojourner Truth Home for Girls.

Mrs. Alexander received National Endowment for the Arts grants to locate former and contemporary designers. She also sought donations of antique dresses and oral histories from wealthy white and black families. She discovered that many dressmakers sewed for someone else and did not have their own labels. Families, however, knew interesting stories of their struggles and achievements. "Most of today's designers told me that they had learned to sew from their mothers and grandmothers. I found many of the older women were still alive. I wanted to talk to them. I wanted to hear their stories and, if possible, obtain some dresses to display in the museum," Mrs. Alexander said.

Luckily, for history, Mrs. Alexander knew the designer Ann Lowe. Ann Lowe designed debutante and wedding dresses for the leading families in America in the 1950s. Mrs. Alexander worked with Ms. Lowe, and she helped Ms. Lowe in her later years, when her health was failing. Mrs. Alexander was a steady force in publicizing Ann's accomplishments and work to the general public.

The Black Fashion Museum is open by appointment. It has a Curator, Board of Directors, monthly programs, and a student showcase-scholarship program. It is also a stop on Heritage Visitor Tours. The museum was recently asked by Bard College, New York, for the loan of a gown by the renowned black designer, Ann Cole Lowe. Ann Lowe created Jackie Kennedy's wedding dress.

The Black Fashion Museum is located at 2007 Vermont Ave., N.W., in Washington, D.C.'s historical district, near the U Street, N.W., restaurant and nightclub area.

Source Material

Alexander, Lois. *The Role of the Negro in Retailing in New York City from 1863 to the Present*. Master's Thesis, 1963.

Harlem's Fashio Museum, article written by Norma Jean Darden, Pp 82-83, November 1997. Personal Interviews with Director Joyce Alexander Bailey, Valerie Chisholm, and Dr. Lenore Cole Alexander.

A Harlem Museum Devoted to Black Fashion Designers, by Vukani Magubane, N.Y. Amsterdam News, April, 1981

Rosemary E. Reed Miller and Sabrina Miller.

About the Author

Rosemary E. Reed Miller first opened Toast and Strawberries on R Street, at Connecticut Ave., N.W., in 1966, and moved around the corner in 1995. The year 1966 was a tough one to open a business in downtown Washington. For an African American woman, it was an act of courage.

Through hard work, determination, and creativity, she and the people who came into the "World of Toast" shaped the store into a very unique gift and fashion apparel shop. Over the years, Toast has served a true cross-section of the metropolitan area, and, because Toast is located in the international Dupont Circle area, Toast has literally served the world. "I chose Dupont Circle because I saw the many hotels, museums, bookstores, and galleries located there," Rosemary said. "In 1966, the area was quite racially and economically mixed. I did not know, however, because I was not from

Family photo: Byron (deceased) and Eloise Reed (deceased), my brother, Byron (deceased), and me. My father was a community activist and science teacher.

My mother, Eloise S. Reed, graduating from University of Pennsylvania in the early 1940s. She was an art and interior design major.

My husband, Paul (deceased), and my children, Sabrina and Paul.

Washington, that blacks did not live and have businesses on the west side of Connecticut Ave. Such are the protocols of black and white America."

She found resistance from landladies to rent to her. She asked the D.C. Office of Human Rights to help. The landladies told the official that they were not discriminating, but they thought she was "too young" to be serious. Rosemary was then in her twenties.

Paul E. Miller, Dean of Howard University Law School, [top photo] lecturing students.

The Miller family: Paul E., Sabrina, Rosemary, and Paul D. Miller.

Rosemary graduated from Temple University in Philadelphia with an A. B. in History and Anthropology. Her focus was on the emerging countries in Africa. "I didn't get the graduate funding to study in Africa, so I thought I could do work on new world Africans. I knew people in Jamaica. I thought I could study there. I ended up writing for newspapers there and in the U.S. I wrote for *Women's Wear Daily*, Fairchild Publications, the *Miami Herald*, the *Miami News*, the *Amsterdam News*, and for the the *Daily Gleaner* in Jamaica. I also started designing and selling clothing and accessories."

Toast and Strawberries has been featured in articles in the *Washington Post*, the *Washington Star*, the *Afro-American*, the Swedish journal, *Dagen Nyeter*, and in such periodicals as *Black Enterprise*, *Essence*, the *Washingtonian*, *Ms. Magazine*, *Glamour*, *Encore*, and the *Washington View*.

Ms. Reed-Miller has served on various service and professional boards: The African American Theatre Company, D.C. Economic Development Commission, Woodley House [mental retardation], Arts Media Services, and Interracial Council on Business Opportunities.

She has been an officer for the Howard University Faculty Wives and the Association of Women Business owners. She was a delegate to the White House Conference on Economic Development and was a member of the Presidential Task Force on Education and Training for Minority Business Enterprises. She is currently vice president of African Travel Associates, and president of her civic organization, Neighbors, Inc.

Many government and civic groups have honored Reed-Miller for her service: National Association of Negro Business and Professional Women's Club, Alpha Kappa Alpha Sorority, Iota Phi Lambda Sorority, BISA Calendar person, the D.C. Chamber of Commerce, and the Association for the Study of African American Life and History.

She has received numerous awards and recognition: Small Business Person of the Year; Small Business Association; Howard University Small Business Development Center; the Business and Professional League, and many others. Reed currently teaches fashion merchandising at Prince George's Community College. She has also taught at the University of the District of Columbia and Howard University. She is listed in *Who's Who Among Black Americans* and in the *Who's Who of Women.*

Television and radio programs often call Ms. Reed Miller to speak or do presentations on timely subjects. She is asked to visit local schools and colleges, to sit on panels, to participate in career conferences, and to conduct fashions shows.

Rosemary was born on June 22, on the cusp of Cancer and Gemini. Cancer, the "home" sign, means that Toast and Strawberries is a shop that gives customers a lot of good "motherly" advice, and "fashion therapy." Gemini—the busy twins and "sun sign"—express themselves in Toast and Strawberries' innovative and multifaceted approach to fashion merchandising, design, and community service.

Rosemary is the daughter of Byron and Eloise Reed of Yeadon, Pennsylvania, a suburb adjacent to Philadelphia. She is the widow of Paul E. Miller, of Dayton, Ohio. Paul was a professor of law and dean of the Howard University School of Law. Dean Miller died in 1974. Rosemary and Paul had two children, Sabrina Eloise and Paul Dennis, and two grandchildren, Kerwince and Hakeem.

The tradition, from Eloise Scott Reed's musical and artistic family, continues with Sabrina, a gourmet cook, who sells real estate, rehabilitates houses, and has studied Vodun in Haiti. Paul, her son, AKA 'D J Spooky', is known in the literary, digital art, sculpture, and music world as "that Subliminal Kid."

Author, Rosemary E. Reed Miller

Epilogue

Over the years, Toast and Strawberries has presented the history and fashion program, *Threads of Time, the Fabric of History*. The program combined narrative vignettes and modeling to give various audiences a sense of the history of African American women in dressmaking and designing since slavery.

Toast and Strawberries displayed examples of how dressmaking had served as an avenue to freedom and self-reliance for African American women slaves. Our research showed that the women had made a decision to improve their lives despite enormous obstacles. The choice to design clothes ultimately led to wider opportunity. It was also intriguing to learn that these women, in almost every case, contributed to their communities through leadership and financial direction.

The same spirit continues among contemporary designers. Some started out just designing clothes, but as they obtained a better financial base, they went on to fine art, as in the case of Joyce Scott; or teaching, as exemplified by Patricia Jackson; or on to accessories, as is the case with Cindy Williams.

Most of the current designers have connected with Toast and Strawberries at some time. It has been a pleasant and rewarding experience to work with these fabulous women. We have learned much from them, and they have exposed our customers to distinctive clothes.

More research is needed to find designers and dressmakers in other cities and across the country. African Americans have talent and have used it throughout the years. It is our goal to expand our discovery of these artists, their work and share them with the world.

Rosemary E. Reed Miller

The Threads of Time, the Fabric of History deserves the attention of everyone interested in celebrating the struggles and accomplishments of African-American dressmakers and designers of the 19th and 20th Century America.

Not only do we read about their lives, but also the people and places they touched. I was most pleased to see that Ms. Reed Miller highlighted Bordentown Training Institute, where my father, William Hastie taught before going on to Harvard Law School, to the deanship at Howard Law School, and to service as the first African-American Federal judge in the United States.

Bordentown attracted talented students and dedicated teachers. The students were taught academic subjects while learning trades such as barbering, shoe making and dressmaking. Also, and maybe most importantly, the Bordentown students were exposed to teachers, who helped them to think logically and strategically, and who were called 'race leaders' in those days, leading the fight for economic and leagl rights for African American citizens.

I recommend this significant book which adds to our shared vision of strong women entrepreneurs in dress designing—a new area of contribution to American history by African-Americans.

Karen Hastie Williams, Esq.

Threads of Time: The Fabric of History reflects just one aspect of Rosemary Reed Miller's lifelong commitment to building bridges between community, fashion, and public art. As one of the most notable and successful African American woman-owned businesses in Washington D.C., Toast and Strawberries shows the same dedication to combining financial independence and community building as the women profiled in the pages of this book. I urge you to buy this book and share it with your families, friends, colleagues, children, grandmothers, aunts, and uncles, or, in other words, anyone you can find who will listen to these remarkable stories of the past and present that are full of the wisdom of individual and collective struggle from those who, like the clothes they design and sew, actually do "make" history, but whom history rarely records as starring players. By bringing together these figures into one book that is accessible to people of all ages and backgrounds, Rosemary Reed Miller provides both an entertaining and informative guide to the contributions of African American women dressmakers and designers to American fashion, politics, and social history. *Threads of Time: The Fabric of History* can serve as an invaluable teaching tool, whether at the kitchen table, the sewing table, or the seminar table. I highly recommend this provocative and insightful book.

Amy Robinson
Department of English
Georgetown University